Maintaining &Repairing

YOUR SCALE MODEL TRAINS

Jim Volhard

KALMBACH
BOOKS

Printed in Canada

05 06 07 08   10 9 8 7 6 5 4 3

Visit our website at
www.kalmbachbooks.com
Secure online ordering available

Publisher's Cataloging-in-Publication
(Provided by Quality Books, Inc.)

Volhard, Jim.
    Maintaining & repairing your scale model trains / Jim
Volhard. —1st ed.
    p. cm.
    Includes bibliographical references and index.
    ISBN: 0-89024-324-7

    1. Railroads–Models–Maintenance and repair. I.
Title. II. Title: Maintaining and repairing your scale
model trains

TF197.V65 1999   625.1'9'0288
                                 QBI98-1293

Book and cover design: Kristi Ludwig

Contents

Introduction

Model railroading is a uniquely fascinating hobby. Our trains are not static miniature displays, as in so many other hobbies, but function like the real thing. Ours is a dynamic hobby. Whether a train is a highly detailed model running through super-realistic scenery or just a small train set running on a loop of track, it has movement and life.

Unfortunately, external forces are constantly at work trying to cover up and render inoperable what we work so hard to create. Dust, dirt, oxidation, dampness, dryness, expansion, contraction, clumsy hands, children, adults who should know better, pets, pests, abuse, wear, and many other problems can affect our miniature world. Fortunately, if modelers follow some basic maintenance and repair procedures, they can prevent many of these potential problems or minimize their effect.

The goal of this book is to provide the model railroader with the basics of model railroad maintenance and repair. It is not a compilation of every method of dealing with every problem that could possibly befall a model railroad. Some ideas and methods may be new to you, and some are old, time-tested procedures. I claim none as original ideas. Maintaining and repairing your model empire may not provide the same sense of accomplishment and source of enjoyment as, say, superdetailing a locomotive or scratchbuilding a unique structure. But having a good maintenance program and repairing items in a timely manner will result in increased enjoyment of the hobby, which is what it is all about.

Tools & Techniques
CHAPTER ONE

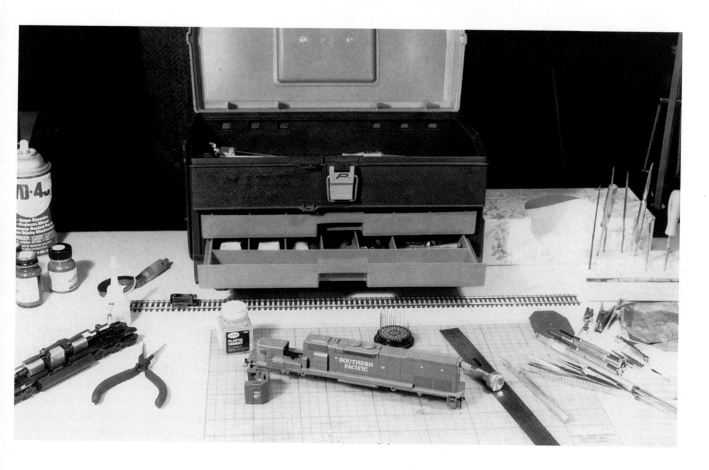

In order to maintain and repair your miniature empire you'll need a few tools and supplies. Fortunately, you can buy many of them as you become more involved in the hobby. Buying tools and supplies as you need them tends to spread the investment over a period of time. While it doesn't decrease the cost, it does usually lower the chance that the purchases will blow your budget. Most hobbyists don't build a large, elaborate layout and then one day decide that they need a trainload of tools. Rather, the tools you use to construct your empire are the ones you'll use to maintain and repair it.

A simple, well-chosen collection of tools that meets most of your basic needs doesn't have to be expensive or take up a lot of room. Many of your modeling tools will also be useful around the house to fix countless household items, a good bargaining point when you need to justify such an expenditure.

WORK AREA

A collection of tools means little without a decent place to work. If you must repair or maintain an item in place, you'll have to make the best of the location at hand. In difficult locations, a little extra time spent in moving things out of harm's way can make the job a little easier. If you can remove the item, you'll be able to do the work in a more suitable location. For model railroading purposes, the same area set aside for modeling can double as a repair and maintenance area. If you have the luxury of ample room, you could set aside a separate area for this purpose. This would eliminate any disruption of ongoing modeling projects. The lead photo shows a modeling workbench that can be used to repair and maintain items.

ESSENTIAL TOOLS AND SUPPLIES

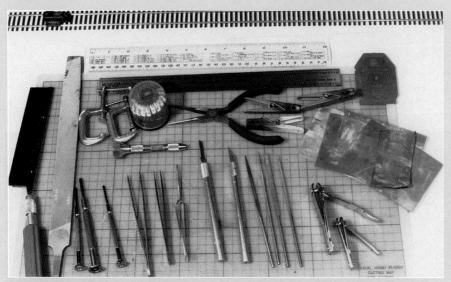

A variety of small tools will aid in maintaining and repairing your scale empire.

Here is a list of the tools and supplies you will use most frequently:

Screwdrivers. You will need two sets of screwdrivers, a miniature set for small items and a regular set for larger applications. A nice set usually includes a variety of flat- and Phillips-head screwdrivers. Be sure to use the right size for the job. Using the wrong-size screwdriver can damage the screwdriver tip or the slot in the screw.

Pliers. Several types would be nice. Conventional and needle-nose types are all useful. A needle-nose with smooth jaws is nice for working with items that could be damaged by the serrations on a normal pair. Adjustable and locking pliers come in handy for larger jobs.

Hammer. A small hammer with a 4- to 6-ounce head would be useful for smaller jobs, while a normal hammer with a 12-ounce head works best for larger jobs.

Wrenches. An assortment of small open or combination wrenches would come in handy. Lacking these, several small adjustable wrenches would do. A ¼" drive socket set would have many uses.

Soldering iron. A small pencil-type soldering iron would do for most modeling jobs. You'll also need flux and several types of solder for various applications.

Side cutter. Xuron makes a good side cutter that is perfect for hobby use. Its hardened jaws will cut all sorts of thin metal and wire. For larger jobs, use a heavier side cutter.

Drill and bits. Here a wide variety is nice. For small jobs, a pin vise and miniature twist drills are a necessity. For larger jobs, an electric drill and a set of ¹⁄₁₆"–⅜" bits are the ticket.

Tap and die. Indispensable for cutting threads. Taps would be the more useful of the two. If you have the bucks you could buy an entire set, but for most people it is more economical to buy just the items you need. Several commonly used sizes are 2-56, 1-72, 0-80, and 00-90.

Clamps. A selection of C clamps and locking pliers has many uses.

Files. A set of needle files and one or two larger mill files have many uses. Be sure to keep the teeth clean. Some plastic and soft metals quickly fill the teeth with debris, resulting in poor or little cutting action. Use a fine wire brush to keep the teeth clean.

Knives. X-acto offers a large variety of blades, handles, and other assorted cutting tools. No. 1 handles are good for light duty. Buy several so you do not have to change blades all the time. The most commonly used blades are no. 11 and no. 17. Check your hobby shop or catalog for more items that many be of use.

Tweezers. A variety of different-size tweezers are great for handling small parts or getting into small places.

Emery cloth and sandpaper are useful items for finishing and polishing. A variety of sizes have many uses. A good item is Flex-i-grit, a flexible plastic material that comes in a variety of grit sizes.

Saws. A number of different saws serve different purposes. Use a jeweler's saw and a razor saw for small items. Use a hacksaw for heavier metal items and a handsaw or power tools for heavier wood items.

Vise. While a vise is not a necessity, it is nice to have access to one to hold items securely while working on them.

Adhesives. You will need a variety of types, each with its own specific use.

   Liquid solvent types to use on plastic.

   Cyanoacrylate (super glue), or CA, for joining dissimilar materials. There are a variety of types of cyanoacrylate for specific needs.

   Wood glue for wood, paper, and other porous materials.

Epoxy for all materials where strength is important.

Silicone seal for a variety of uses when you need flexibility.

Measuring tools. A variety of rulers will be useful. You'll need both conventional (U.S. and metric) and scale rulers. In model railroading an NMRA gauge is the ultimate tool for track and wheel measurement. Exotic but useful items would be a micrometer and calipers for exact measurement. While top-end instruments are very expensive, there are some lower-priced items that cost under $10 and work well for most modeling applications.

Lubricants. The number of lubricants you'll need depends on what equipment you run. For model railroading, Labelle makes an extensive line of lubricants that should meet most modeling needs. They include motor and gear oil, some that are plastic compatible, and a powdered Teflon material that works well in couplers. Another lubricant that has many uses is WD-40. This product can be used as a light lubricant, a cleaning solvent, and a penetrating oil to free sticking and rusted parts.

Miscellaneous. Scissors and knives, as well as many other household and shop items too numerous to mention will be of use. Need will dictate what items to use.

When you do purchase tools, try to buy high-quality items. Avoid "bargain bin" tools. While they may look as good as the more expensive tools, you get what you pay for. Consider tools an investment that, with proper care, will last a long time. More tools are ruined by improper use than are worn out actually doing what they are intended to do.

Fig. 1-1. Have an area set aside to store all your parts and supplies. Organize and label everything, or you will spend more time looking for a thing than fixing it.

Lacking space for a dedicated area, you can use the nomadic approach. Any available table will do—just be sure to protect the surface you are working on. A nasty stain or scratch on the kitchen table could seriously upset domestic tranquility. And clean up after yourself.

Adequate lighting should be available, regardless of location. You cannot work on something you cannot see. At the workbench, an inexpensive swing-arm lamp will work fine. A portable lamp is great for tables and other such locations. In odd places such as under a layout, a "trouble light" or one of those movable painting lights will do fine.

Another aid, especially if you are working with small parts, is a low-power optical visor. Even if your vision is good, the extra magnification can be helpful in locating trouble and reducing eyestrain.

Having tools is one thing, but locating them can be another. Nothing is more frustrating than searching for items that you know exist in your home but cannot be found. A good idea is a small toolbox that will hold many of these items. Whether you

keep it in your layout area or in some other convenient location in your home doesn't matter, as long as you can find it. Become a stickler about returning tools to the box when you are finished with them, and insist that everyone in the house does the same.

SUPPLY STORAGE

It is amazing what a model railroader can accumulate in the way of parts and supplies. After a period of time it is not only a good idea to organize your inventory, it is a necessity. If you don't, you will spend more time looking for things than using them. Figure 1-1 shows several small drawer organizers for small parts and a chest of drawers for larger items, all labeled for their contents. Size your storage area according to your needs and, again, be a stickler about returning items to their proper place when you are finished with them.

WORKING SAFELY

For all the relaxation and enjoyment that model railroading provides, it can also be dangerous. While it's not likely to be dangerous in the sense of causing great bodily harm, there are many smaller potential dangers that could cause problems to you and those around you. The work area of the typical modeler is a potential household hazard and should be treated as such.

In the course of modeling, maintaining, and repairing you'll work with sharp tools, solvents, hot soldering irons, electrical components with potentially dangerous voltage, and some power tools. For the most part, simple common sense is all that is needed. You probably do not need a list of dos and don'ts posted by your work area, but be sure to follow any manufacturer's recommendations regarding the use of their products. Use care when working with sharp, hot, or moving power tools. Use adequate ventilation and a mask or respirator when working with paints and solvents that produce strong odors. The problem with solvents is that their effects may not be immediate but they can accumulate in the body and cause problems down the road.

Seek professional help when dealing with high-voltage electricity unless you know exactly what you are doing. Use eye protection when working with power tools or in any situation when there is the slightest chance of flying debris.

Not only your own safety is at risk, but that of your family and anyone else who might have access to your work area. Keep solvents, sharp tools, and small parts out of reach especially if you have small children or if they visit frequently. A moment of carelessness may lead to a lifetime of regret.

ESSENTIAL TECHNIQUES

In the course of your modeling projects you will work with many different tools and materials. The ability to work with these tools and materials will determine the success or failure of a maintenance or repair project, so here are a few essential techniques that you'll definitely want to practice.

Filing. After cutting and sawing, filing is the next most efficient way to remove material. When filing a flat surface, use the largest file you can. This serves two purposes. It allows efficient removal of material and will more likely result in a true and flat surface. Filing large items works better if you can clamp the part in a vise or hold it stationary in some way so that you can use two hands on the file (fig. 1). As a result, the pressure applied to the surface will be more even. On small parts one hand is usually sufficient to control the file. Hold your work and file firmly and use as long a stroke as possible (fig. 2). Whether using one hand or two, try to keep even pressure on your work and check your progress often.

Files are cutting tools and like all cutting tools they become dull with use. When this happens throw them out. A dull file is inefficient and frustrating to use. But do not confuse a dull file with one that is

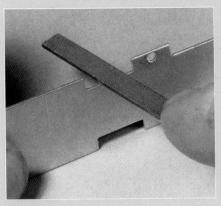

Fig. 2. You can hold needle files in one hand. If possible, position your index finger farther up the file to give better control and more even pressure.

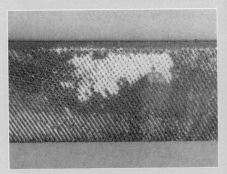

Fig. 3. File teeth may be plugged with plastic or soft metal. Use a wire brush to remove the material and restore cutting action. When a file no longer cuts decently even when clean, throw it away and buy a new one.

Fig. 1. When filing a large object, secure it firmly. Use both hands on the file so you can make smooth, even strokes. This will give you better control of the file and remove the excess material most efficiently.

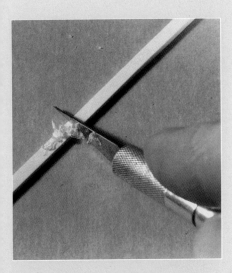

Fig. 4. Scraping is an efficient way to remove plastic and wood in confined areas or on irregularly shaped objects.

Fig. 5. When you're sanding plastic, it is best to use water. This wet-sanding will keep the removed material from clogging the grit. When sanding metal, use a light oil for the same purpose.

simply clogged with material (fig. 3). Remove the offending material with a small wire brush.

Scraping. Scraping is similar to filing, except you're using a nearly perpendicular knife blade to remove material. This is a useful method when there is little or no room to use a file. Hold the knife blade at about a 90 degree angle to the surface and start scraping away the unneeded material (fig. 4). Different styles of X-acto blades may come in handy for different scraping applications. Stop scraping when the material is nearly removed, and finish the area with sandpaper.

Sanding. Sanding is the final finishing process. It reduces the size of the imperfections on models to a point where they become inconsequential or invisible. My favorite sanding medium is Flex-i-grit, made by K&S Engineering. I hesitate to call it sandpaper because it has a flexible plastic backing instead of paper. Emery cloth is another useful product, but the thickness of the cloth backing does

not allow the control of Flex-i-grit. An "A" pack of Flex-i-grit contains five sheets of assorted grades from coarse to superfine for finishing. Another sanding tool is the X-acto sanding stick, mentioned previously in the tool section. It uses narrow belts of sandpaper material in various grit sizes that mount on a plastic "stick." It is a handy item for sanding in confined areas. You can do the same thing by wrapping sandpaper around a stick, but the ease of use more than justifies owning a sanding stick.

To sand styrene or any plastic

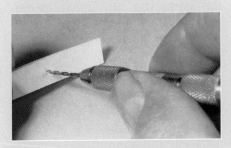

Fig. 6. Use a slow speed to drill. High speeds will melt plastic, and it's more efficient to drill metal at low speeds.

material, use a process called wet-sanding. Wet the sandpaper or part with a small amount of water before you start to sand. The water keeps the sanded-off plastic material from clogging the grit. In effect it is a kind of lubricant (fig. 5). Attempting to sand without water is very inefficient. You have to continually wipe or shake the clogged grit from the sandpaper.

The sanding process begins with selecting the proper grit size. Which grit you choose depends on the condition of the surface to be sanded. A rough and irregular surface requires a coarse grit to remove material quickly. When you reach the proper shape, switch to the next-finer grade and continue sanding. Do not switch to the next-finer grade until you have removed the scratches from the previous grade. Continue this process down to the finest sheet. If you do it properly, a super finish will result that blends in perfectly with the surrounding area. If when sanding is complete there are low spots, cracks or other blemishes, rework the area by filling, filing, and repeating the sanding process. Remember, this is the final finished surface. Paint will not cover flaws visible to the naked eye.

Drilling. Drilling is a rather simple operation—not too many rules or

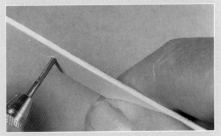

Fig. 7. It's best to do tapping by hand. Use firm downward pressure to start the tap. Once the threads have engaged you can reduce pressure—turning the tap will continue cutting the threads. Use a light oil as a lubricant when tapping metal.

tricks here. Two things to keep in mind are: Use sharp bits, and keep the speed low. A sharp bit will produce a springlike coil of cut material when turned (fig. 6). Dull bits are best thrown away—they are not that expensive. Small bits are quite fragile, so use light pressure and keep the bit properly aligned. Excess side pressure is often fatal to them. Keeping the speed low is not a problem when you're using a hand-held pin vise. When you're using a bit in a power drill, though, excess speed will cause plastic around the hole to soften and melt.

Tapping. This is the process of cutting threads for a screw into a previously drilled hole. It is a straightforward operation. Use a chart that shows the proper size hole to drill for the tap you will use. After drilling the hole, chuck the tap in the pin vise and begin to turn the tap into the hole, making sure the tap is aligned with the hole (fig. 7). After several turns, back the tap out and clean the debris off the tap. Repeat this operation until you completely sink the threads on the tap. Plastic is much softer than metal, so take care not to strip the threads when cutting them. The hole is now ready to accept the screw.

Soldering. Soldering is a simple operation in which certain nonferrous metals are joined by heating a soft metal called solder to a molten state. This molten metal flows between the mating surfaces and cools, forming a strong

Fig. 8. When soldering two objects together, make sure that both surfaces are clean and that you have removed all dirt and oxidation. Apply flux to the joint to help the solder flow into the joint.

Fig. 10. As the solder melts, continue holding the iron until the solder flows completely into the joint or covers the wires. Then remove the iron.

Fig. 9. Heat the parts and hold the solder away from the tip of the soldering iron. The heat of the parts should melt the solder.

Fig. 11. After removing the iron, do not move the parts until the solder has cooled enough to set. You can recognize this liquid-to-solid transformation when the solder's surface, previously bright and shiny, becomes frosted.

joint. For modeling purposes, metals including brass, copper, and nickel-silver are all easy to solder.

The soldering process is quite easy. First, clean the parts to be joined of any dirt and tarnish. Apply a small amount of petroleum-jelly-like material called soldering flux to the intended joints (fig. 8). Use a heat source such as a soldering iron or small torch to heat the parts (fig. 9). Touch solder, which comes in wire form, to the parts to be joined. When the parts are hot enough, the solder melts and flows into the joint (fig. 10). Finally, remove the heat source. When the joint cools sufficiently,

the solder will return to a solid state, as indicated by a slightly frosty appearance, and the joint is complete (fig. 11).

Soldering has many applications in model railroading. The most common use is for wiring railroads. Solder provides a hard, solid, highly conductive joint between track components, wire, and the power source. Use a rosin-core solder for all electrical connections. Soldering is used almost exclusively to construct those imported brass engines. In model detailing it has limited use unless the modeler is building up brass parts. It is used more for wiring in model locomotives.

Maintaining & Repairing
Diesel Locomotives

CHAPTER TWO

Model railroaders can walk into any well-stocked hobby shop and buy a ready-to-run locomotive that not only looks great but runs like a fine watch. The skills required are no more difficult than opening a box and placing the unit on the rails. Unfortunately, the moment the unit turns a wheel, outside forces begin to act on the locomotive. Some basic skills are required to maintain that locomotive so it continues to run like new, or to fix it in the event of some mechanical problem.

Before going any further it is worth the time for beginners and even those with some experience to take Diesel Locomotive 101. Here you'll first learn basic locomotive terminology, so we all speak the same language; then you'll explore basic mechanical and electrical principles, so you know what makes your model work. One note here: Manufacturers may have slightly different names for the same basic part. Study the locomotive instructions and exploded view to see if any difference exists. Although it may not make any differ-

ence what you call a part, if you have to contact the manufacturer for any reason it helps to use the same name they do for each part.

BASIC LOCOMOTIVE COMPONENTS AND TERMINOLOGY

While there are many different locomotive models on the market made by a number of manufacturers, almost all units share the same basic construction and components.

Exterior components. The body of the typical diesel locomotive model, whether it is made of plastic, cast metal, or brass, is only there for cosmetic reasons. On a few models, the body serves as a mounting base for the couplers, but that is the only mechanical function it serves. Operating details such as spinning fan blades, operating lights, or other animated features are present for purely aesthetic reasons and do not contribute to the mechanical operation of the locomotive. Figure 2-1 shows a

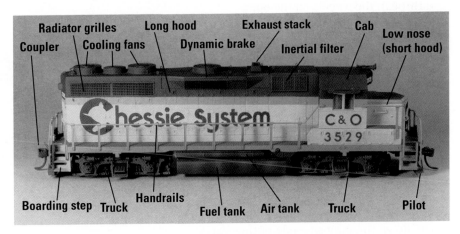

Fig. 2-1. A typical diesel roadswitcher, identifying the major external components

typical road-switcher-type locomotive with the most important external features identified.

Mechanical components. The guts of an operational model diesel locomotive lie under the body. The chassis is the mechanical heart of the locomotive, similar to what would be left if you removed the body from an automobile. Besides any remaining cosmetic details such as the truck sideframes and the fuel tank, this is where the electrical energy is picked up from the track and converted into mechanical motion. Figure 2-2 shows a typical chassis with the major components identified, and fig. 2-3 is an exploded view of the major components with the parts identified.

Electrical components. Although the basic mechanical components are important to the operation of a locomotive, they are useless unless the electricity that powers the locomotive has a path to the motor. While it is not rocket science, locomotive manufacturers have devised ingenious ways to route power from the rails to the motor with an eye toward keeping the components as unobtrusive as possible. Figure 2-4 shows an electrical schematic of the typical model locomotive. At first glance, the exploded view of the drive components in fig. 2-3 may not make electrical sense. But if you follow the electrical path from the wheels on one side of the locomotive to the motor and through the wheels on the opposite side of the locomotive, the mystery should clear up. In essence, each half of the locomotive truck, including the wheels, is electrically separate from the other half. The current picked up from the wheels on one side passes through the truck and is routed by wire to one of the motor terminals. After passing through the motor, the current leaves through the other terminal that is attached to the frame. From the frame the current passes through the pivot point of the truck, down the opposite side of the truck back to the wheels, and into the

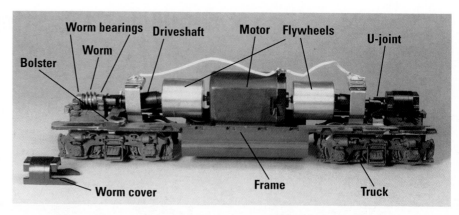

Fig. 2-2. A typical model diesel chassis, identifying the major components

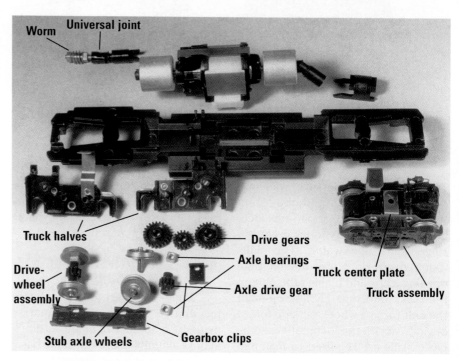

Fig. 2-3. Chassis broken down with smaller parts identified

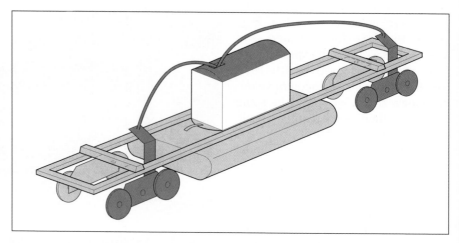

Fig. 2-4. Electrical schematic of a typical model diesel locomotive

opposite rail, completing the circuit. Knowing how electricity flows through the locomotive will be helpful when you're adding accessories or dealing with problems.

INSPECTING NEW DIESEL LOCOMOTIVES

Manufacturers such as Kato, Atlas, and Life-Like Proto 2000 have given us top-of-the-line performance right out of the box. About the only work necessary to put new motive power on your layout is to install the proper couplers and add the small detail parts. While there is nothing wrong with running a locomotive right out of the box, it can be worthwhile to check "under the hood" of a new unit.

Begin your inspection by removing the body from the chassis and look for obvious problems. While most manufacturers have rigid quality control and test-run locomotives before they leave the factory, a part may work loose or—very rarely—be broken in shipping. Hold the chassis and swivel the trucks to make sure they move freely.

Check to make sure the locomotive has been lubricated. It is much more likely that the locomotive has been overlubricated than under. The lubrication is easily seen as "wet" areas around the truck and motor. Use a tissue to wipe off all the excess lubricant that you can reach. The excess lubricant does not benefit the drive train and only attracts dirt, which will cause problems down the road. A complete guide to lubrication appears later in this chapter.

While the body is off, set your locomotive on the rails and run it. Here is a chance to check all the moving parts for potential problems. One of the more common problems that could occur—but still rare—is that one of the driveshafts may not be connected. It is easy to connect the loose end to the proper drive component. If you find everything running as it should, replace the body and install your couplers if they

DISASSEMBLING DIESEL LOCOMOTIVES

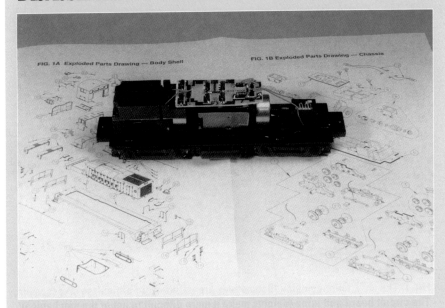

Many instruction sheets include an exploded view of the locomotive. This is a valuable tool when you're disassembling a locomotive or when you need repair parts.

To do anything beyond cleaning wheels, you'll have to learn how to disassemble a locomotive. The best source of information on disassembly is the instruction sheet. If it has specific instructions, use them. If not, you must do a little detective work to figure out how to remove the shell.

You'll have to remove the couplers of some units first. If the couplers are mounted on the chassis or frame and the pilots on the shell have no slots to allow the coupler to pass while the body is removed, the couplers will have to be removed. Couplers usually are secured with a clip, pin, or screw. Determine which by observation or by referring to the exploded view of the unit, and remove the couplers accordingly.

On most plastic diesels some form of molded-on tab or clip holds the body in place. If the instruction sheet has no disassembly procedure, refer to the exploded view of the locomotive. It will probably give you

clues about the location of the securing devices. On some units small buttons or ridges are cast into the chassis. The body has corresponding holes, tabs, or grooves into which these protrusions fit when the body is in place. To remove such a body, you'll have to pry the body shell gently away from the chassis, far enough to clear the protrusions, and lift off the shell. Older Athearn, Atlas, and some N scale units use this system.

Newer Athearn units have four lugs that extend from the bottom of the shell and fit into corresponding openings in the chassis in the fuel tank area. To remove one of these shells, grasp the fuel tank with one hand, squeeze the middle of the hood together slightly with the other hand over the location of the tab, and wiggle until the body works loose. If the body fails to loosen, use a screwdriver and push on the ends of the tabs, which are visible at the bottom of the fuel

Fig. 1. The new, more complex locomotives are a little more difficult to disassemble. The circuit board and large weights make it more difficult to get at the mechanical components for adjustment or maintenance.

Fig. 2. When the large weight is removed, everything is much more accessible. Most wiring that leads to a circuit board is attached using some type of clip. When removing any wires, make a note of their position or return them to their proper position as soon as you finish your work so you do not forget where they go.

tabs that hook onto the chassis, but they are much more accessible than the Atlas or Kato tabs. The only drawback is that it is quite easy to break them off, so use care not to bend them too much.

Brass locomotive bodies are attached to their chassis with screws. These screws are usually located under the unit near the ends and in the area of the fuel tank.

Once the body is removed, there may be more obstacles before you can get to the mechanical components. Extra weights and lighting or circuit boards may be in the way (fig. 1). In the case of N scale units the weight may be an integral part of the chassis. Again, follow the instructions given to remove any of these components. If none are included, use the exploded diagram again to decipher how these parts are secured. Most lighting circuit boards have some type of plug or some way to remove the wires without unsoldering anything. If you are dealing with individual wires, make a diagram showing how they are located before removing them so you can relocate them properly later.

With weights and electronics out of the way (fig. 2), the mechanical meat of the chassis should now be accessible. You can remove the trucks on many HO scale locomotives by removing the worm gear cover, because it doubles as the truck retainer. Then lift out the worm gear and pull the driveshaft apart. You can now remove the trucks.

To remove the wheels or access the gears in the truck on many plastic locomotives you now must remove the gear case clips. You can usually pry them off with a small screwdriver.

tank. Doing this should loosen it adequately.

Kato and Atlas bodies can be difficult to remove. These units have smaller tabs that extend from the body and lock onto the chassis. These tabs are usually located near the trucks. To loosen them you must get a small screwdriver or similar tool between the tab and the chassis and pull on the body to remove it.

Other manufacturers may have different variations on the same theme. Life-Like Proto 2000 road-switcher locomotives have small

Fig. 2-5. Check all locomotive wheels for correct gauge before operation.

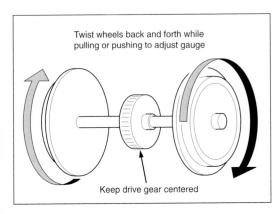

Twist wheels back and forth while pulling or pushing to adjust gauge

Keep drive gear centered

Fig. 2-6. Adjust the wheels by twisting them in or out until they fit perfectly in the slots. Be sure to keep the drive gear centered between the wheels.

do not come installed. With your unit on the rails use an NMRA gauge to check coupler and trip pin height and coupler movement. If you have to make any coupler changes or adjustments, refer to that section later in this chapter.

Check the wheel gauge. Using the NMRA standards gauge, check the depth and fit of the wheel flanges in the notches provided. The flanges should fit perfectly into the notches

as shown in figs. 2-5 and 2-6. If you do find wheels that are out of gauge, you'll have to adjust them for reliable operation. This is rather easy on Athearn units. Just remove the bottom gear box clip on the truck, and you'll be able to remove the wheels. On Kato and Atlas units you'll have to remove the body first. Use a small screwdriver or similar tool to reach down from the top between the frame and the truck to remove the axle retainer.

To adjust the wheel gauge, simply twist the wheel on the axle and either push in or pull out. When it is dead on, roll the axle assembly on a flat surface to make sure the wheels are square with the axle and do not wobble. After any wheel gauge adjustment, make sure that the axle drive gear is still centered between the wheels, or you may have problems when you're trying to return the axle to the truck. Return the wheels to the truck and replace the axle retainer.

The depth of the wheel flanges should not exceed the depth of the notches in the gauge. This is not a problem on newer locomotives, since these manufacturers' wheels conform to the NMRA specifications. Some older locomotives, however, may have deep-flange wheels. Those deep flanges will "bottom out" when crossing switch and crossing frogs, causing the locomotive to bounce over those track components. Not only is this aesthetically undesirable, it can cause electrical contact problems. The edge of the flange may also be sharp, not rounded. This will make the wheel more likely to "pick a switch point" or catch on any track imperfection. If you have such a locomotive, you should change the wheels or you will have constant problems. Better yet, get rid of the entire chassis. Many of these older chassis are not worth saving, anyway.

Check the couplers. Most HO scale locomotives still come with that monstrosity called the NMRA, hornhook, or X2F coupler. This single item is probably the greatest source of frustration for the beginner. If you insist on using these couplers, at least check the height and adjust the uncoupling pin. Check the height with the NMRA gauge. Set the track gauge side onto the track. The rectangular opening in the gauge is the correct height for the long "horn" of the coupler. There is a little leeway here. As long as the height does not vary by more than $\frac{1}{32}''$ either way, you should be all right. If the height needs adjustment, the easiest way is to bend the coupler shank. The couplers have some give, so bend them beyond the adjustment you need. They will spring back most of the way but will retain some of the bend. Do this until the horn is at the correct height. The other adjustment is to the uncoupling pin that hangs down from the shank. In theory these pins are used in conjunction with a "between the rails" uncoupler. Realistically speaking, they are

Fig. 2-7. HO scale X2F coupler shown next to a Kadee gauge. Note the trip pin clearing a thin piece of styrene placed over the rails.

Fig. 2-8. Athearn coupler pad filed flat, drilled, and tapped for a 2-56 screw to mount a Kadee coupler.

the coupler mounting box or coupler end and spring for flash or foreign material and remove any that you find. If this doesn't help, replace the coupler with a different one. With these adjustments these couplers should at least be usable and not cause as many problems.

If you plan to get beyond the "train set" layout you should seriously consider upgrading the couplers. Some manufacturers recognize that many modelers, at least those buying the top-of-the-line units, replace the couplers anyway and include knuckle-type couplers. Until recently Kadee couplers were considered the standard and only worthwhile replacement for the X2F couplers. The company has an extensive line of couplers to fit a variety of different applications. Kadee's patents have expired and a number of other manufacturers have now entered the market, offering similar couplers that are compatible with Kadee's.

Installing Kadee or any other manufacturer's knuckle-type couplers is quite easy on newer locomotives, since many manufacturers have included properly sized coupler boxes. Kadee has an extensive coupler conversion list in the Walthers catalogs that will greatly aid the modeler in choosing the correct coupler for a particular locomotive. The most important consideration is choosing the proper length coupler shank. If you are adding a plow to the pilot, you will need a longer shank to clear the plow for proper operation.

What happens when the locomotive does not have a coupler box that allows installation of new couplers? This scenario is true of all Athearn locomotives released before the C44-9Ws. The modeler has two options here. The first option is to drill and tap a hole in the mounting base for a 2-56 screw (fig. 2-8) and mount the new coupler. The other option, and the one I personally prefer, is to mount the couplers to the body. This is done by stacking usually five

impractical. At the very least, trim these pins so that they do not hang below the top of the railhead. They will snag turnouts and crossings. Lay the NMRA gauge across the tops of the rails and push the car up to the gauge. If the pin clears the gauge, you are fine (fig. 2-7). If it

snags, trim it until it clears. The best way is to remove the pin entirely if you don't plan to use a track-mounted uncoupler.

Check coupler motion as well. The coupler should swing easily to the side and return to its coupled position when released. If not, check pieces of Evergreen .040 ¼″ tile behind the pilots and securing them with liquid cement. Assemble a coupler of your choice and set it in place on the new pad. Mark, drill, and tap a hole for a 2-56 screw to hold the coupler in place. Figure 2-9 shows such an installation. Set the unit on the chassis and check for proper coupler height. If the coupler is too low, remove some material; if it is too high, add some more. Using this method also allows the modeler to close up the pilot area, since the coupler no longer has to slide out of this area.

In N scale, Rapido and Micro-Trains couplers are the only game in town. Most N scale equipment comes with Rapido couplers. This is a workable system. Its biggest disadvantage is its grossly out-of-scale size compared to the Micro-Trains. Other than that, it can be coupled and uncoupled decently, is very strong and reliable, and does not need much adjustment. Several items should be checked to make sure your Rapido couplers operate properly. Be sure that the uncoupling pin does not extend below the rails or it will snag trackwork. If the pin does hang too low, trim off part of it until it clears the rail. The other thing to check is the ease of movement or the ease with which one coupler rides up over another to couple. Use a small screwdriver and lift the coupler. The coupler should move easily and not lift the car wheels from the rails. If the coupler does not move easily, check for flash or other foreign material. If you don't find any, remove the truck from the body and remove the coupler by twisting the shank 90 degrees and lifting it out the top of the coupler box. Be careful not to lose the spring. Check for flash on the coupler shank and in the coupler box and reassemble. These steps are shown in photographs in Chapter Four on rolling stock.

Micro-Trains is the next step up. It offers a number of coupler-mount-

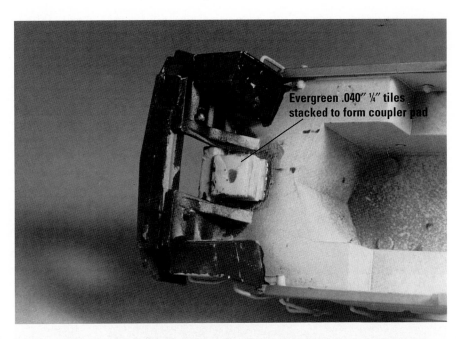

Evergreen .040″ ¼″ tiles stacked to form coupler pad

Fig. 2-9. Rather than use the existing coupler pad on the Athearn frame, build up the pad with styrene squares, then drill and tap it for a 2-56 screw. Mounting the couplers in this manner allows you to fill in the lower pilot slots.

Micro-Trains coupler kit

Fig. 2-10. Micro-Trains makes installation of its N scale couplers on many locomotives easy. It offers kits that fit the pilot openings, such as this example installed on an Atlas GP7.

ing styles that will fit most needs. It also offers coupler conversion kits that will fit a number of popular N scale locomotives. Figure 2-10 shows an example mounted in an Atlas GP7. Just follow Micro-Trains' instructions and make sure the coupler is properly adjusted so it will work reliably.

Test-run the locomotive. If everything looks as you think it should, run the unit for several minutes in different directions and at varying speeds. Check for smooth motion in both the drive train and trucks. If you find excess lubricant around gear cases and the motor area, wipe it off. This excess will not benefit the locomotive and will only collect dirt. If everything is to your liking, you can put the unit in service or go on to add any detail and weathering you wish.

Fig. 2-11. Dirty wheels are the biggest single operational problem on model locomotives.

Fig. 2-12. My favorite method of cleaning wheels involves applying a little WD-40 to the end of a paper towel. Lay the towel across the track and run the locomotive through it. The dirt will dissolve and be deposited on the towel.

MAINTAINING DIESEL LOCOMOTIVES

Like any machine that has moving parts, your model locomotives will need periodic maintenance to keep running well. How much and what type of maintenance depends on how and where you operate your locomotives. If your layout is located in a spare room or a clean basement, the dust and dirt encountered by your locomotive will be minimal. A workshop or garage where there is more dirt and dust will cause a buildup of those materials on both the outside surfaces and the mechanical components. Garden layouts or any type of outside operation will have a whole host of new problems. The usual dirt and dust will be blown by wind and find their way into the drive train much more easily. Moisture or wet conditions can cause rust and corrosion on a much larger scale than even in a damp basement, resulting in greater mechanical and electrical problems. Probably the worst place to run your locomotives is on a carpet or hard floor. Many beginners getting their first train set probably have no choice. It is the only open space available. The biggest enemy here is the dirt, carpet fuzz, and hair. Regardless of how well the carpet is vacuumed or the floor is cleaned, these items will find their way into your locomotives. Dirt and dust will quickly find the lubricant and gum it up, while hair and fuzz will get wrapped around axles and shafts, causing all sorts of problems.

There are a number of things to check on a regular basis. Check the wheel treads for dirt and the mechanism for proper lubrication and dirt buildup. Check the wheels for proper gauge and the couplers for proper height and operation.

Keep the wheels clean. The most often-performed and important part of maintaining your locomotive will be cleaning the wheels. The best, most expensive locomotive cannot run decently unless its wheels are clean. It has always been important to have clean wheels. It has become even more important for those who use DCC control systems, because the carrier signals must be received by the decoder inside the locomotive.

Dirt on wheels is not hard to detect. If you notice your locomotive's headlight beginning to flicker, or if the unit hesitates or stalls, it is time to take a look. Although you can limp along for a while, this condition is chronic and will have to be dealt with. Your problem can be anything from a dull haze to a dark streak along the inside edge of the wheel near the flange (fig. 2-11), and you'll have to remove it.

There are a number of ways to clean wheels. You can scrape off the crud with a knife or with a small wire brush in a motor tool. Kadee makes a neat item called a Loco Driver Cleaner. It is a small wire brush connected to track voltage. The two sides are opposite polarity, so when the brush is touched to the drivers, the voltage spins the locomotive's wheels, and the wire brush removes the dirt. My personal favorite is to remove the crud with WD-40 solvent-lubricant on a piece of paper towel. Spray a little WD-40 on the end of a paper towel and lay it across a piece of track. Be sure to push the towel down between the rails so that the coupler trip pin does not snag it. Run the locomotive onto the part of the towel on which you applied the WD-40. When it stops, leave the power on, pull it back onto the bare track, and let go again. After the first pass or two the dirt should begin coming off the wheels. Move the towel a little so the wheels run over clean towel. When no more dirt comes off the wheels, turn the towel to a dry section with no WD-40. Run the locomotive onto it several more times to dry the wheels. Then take the towel and wipe the dissolved dirt off the track. With a little practice you should be able to clean a set of wheels in less than a minute. Figure 2-12 shows this setup. The beauty of this method is that it involves less handling of the locomotive than others. It would be a good idea to have a wheel-cleaning track. This need be nothing more than a board with a couple of feet of track that can be hooked to a power pack—or you could work a maintenance track into your layout so you would not have to remove your locomotive from the layout.

Lubricate mechanical components. The subject of lubrication will probably yield as many opinions as there are modelers. Most modern model locomotive drive trains are made of a very hard and slippery engineering plastic. They do not need much lubrication at all. The metal-to-metal bearings (motor and worm gear) do need some oil, but that is about it. Dirt is more of a culprit in poor locomotive performance than lack of lubricant. Over a period of time dirt and dust will accumulate in any lubricant. This thickens the lubricant. As the liquid components of the oil and grease slowly evaporate, the residue be-

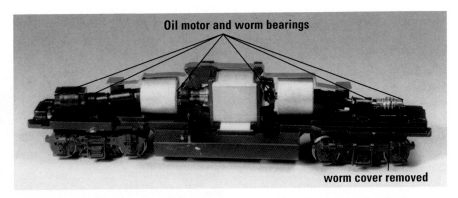

Fig. 2-13. The major lube points on the top side of an Athearn chassis are shown here.

Fig. 2-14. Lower truck lubrication points are shown here.

comes steadily thicker. Adding more lubricant will loosen everything up, but the cycle will repeat itself more quickly as the remaining crud contaminates the new lubricant. Locomotive performance will slowly degrade as the cycle repeats.

All discussion and theory aside, the trick is to put the proper amount of the proper lubricant where it is needed. Most new units come from the factory literally dripping with lubricant. If you really want to do it right, you should tear down the entire drive train and start over. This also applies to used units that have an accumulation of crud. Start with a clean slate.

Tearing down the drive train is not a difficult process. If you haven't

done this before, it is a good idea to study the parts diagram that came with your unit. Then you will have some idea of what to expect. Start by removing the motor from the chassis. If there is any excess oil on the motor or flywheel area, wipe it off and set it aside. Next, remove the trucks from the chassis. Removing the truck retainer clip will also expose the worm gear assembly. Remove these gears carefully so you do not lose any of the bearings or washers and set them aside.

Now you can remove the trucks. One note here: Mark the lead truck and trailing truck as well as the front and rear of each individual truck. If the trucks are reversed when you reassemble everything, the unit will run backward with regard to your throttle. Now remove the truck sideframes. On Athearn and similar units, you can gently pry off the sideframes. Remove the bottom gear box clip and then remove the axles. Remove the top clip, and you'll be able to split the truck, exposing the drive gears.

On Kato and Atlas units, you'll have to remove the axle retainer by prying gently on the tabs. With the retainer off, you can remove the sideframes. Spread the wheels' wipers and remove the axles. Two screws hold the Kato gear case assembly together. Remove them to expose the drive gears.

The inside of the gear cases will most likely be an oily mess. Use warm, soapy water and wash the oil from all drive parts, including the worm drive and universal joints. Set everything aside to dry. When everything has dried, reassemble the gear cases but leave the wheels off.

While the choice of lubricants is up to each individual, I personally prefer Labelle lubricants. They are an extensive line of products that meet almost all needs. Most important, several of the lubricants are plastic-compatible. While you could use almost any light oil, over time some of them react with some plastics, causing softening or brittleness.

In the smaller scales Labelle 108 Plastic Compatible Motor Oil is a good choice for motor, axle, and worm bearings. Only a small drop on each bearing will do the job. Figure 2-13 shows the oil lubrication points of a typical chassis and fig. 2-14 shows the oil lubrication points of a typical truck.

For the gear train, use Labelle 102 Plastic Compatible Gear Lubricant or Labelle 106 Plastic Compatible Grease with Teflon. Apply a small dab to one or two gears in the gear train, shown in fig. 2-15. Running the locomotive will distribute the lubricant.

For larger scale models in which higher torque is produced, use

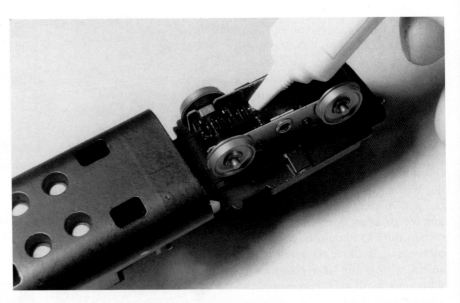

Fig. 2-15. Use a heavier gear oil or gear grease as shown here. Apply only a small dab. Running the unit will distribute the grease evenly to all gears.

Fig. 2-16. Check the drive gears for flash or foreign material. Look carefully at the teeth and along the edge of the center bore.

Labelle 107. This is a medium-weight plastic-compatible motor oil better suited to the larger units.

After lubrication, leave the body off and run your units for several minutes to distribute the lubricant. After running, check for excess lubricant and wipe off any you find. Your unit is now ready for service.

Frequency of lubrication is a function of use. When you note a decline in performance and the wheels are clean, check the bearings. If they are dry or if you can barely detect any lubricant, apply a small drop. Just remember that a little goes a long way. The less you use, the less often you will gum up the works.

There are times when a locomotive will just not run well. The wheels have been cleaned, the mechanism is freshly lubricated, and everything seems to be in good adjustment, but performance just isn't what it used to be or (for new units) what it should be. Maybe it is time to look deeper.

In the case of new units, sometimes the mechanism needs a little tweaking. This seems to be a problem with some Athearn or similar moderately priced units, although even more expensive units can have this problem. I'm not picking on Athearn here but merely stating a fact. One Athearn unit will run well right out of the box while the next may not run nearly as well. What gives? Well, for starters, when I buy an Atlas or Kato locomotive that costs around $100, I expect it to run well right out of the box. When I buy an Athearn unit at half the cost or less I do not expect as much. A common problem with new Athearn units is that their running seems to be "tight" or "stiff." Often just running the unit will loosen the mechanism. If the tightness doesn't bother you, just run the unit and the tightness will very likely remedy itself. If, however, you want immediate improvement, you will have to tear down the unit and inspect the drive train piece by piece.

Tearing down a drive train is not difficult. I explained it earlier in this chapter. If you are new at this, refer to the exploded view of the unit on the Athearn parts list to get an idea of what you will encounter. After taking everything apart, wash all parts in warm, soapy water to remove the lubricant and let the parts dry.

Start with the driveshafts. Check that they telescope into each other properly without binding. Also check how the yoke fits on the ball. Sometimes the yoke fits too tightly on the ball. Remove the shaft and open the yoke by bending the sides

WORKBENCH TIP: Smooth Operation That Brings a Bright, White Smile to Your Face

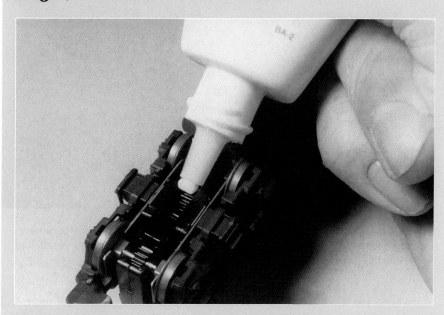

You can hasten the wearing-in of a locomotive by replacing the lubricant with a mild abrasive. Apply some Pearl Drops tooth polish to the drive gears. The abrasive will wear the sharpness off the new gears and should result in smoother operation.

Talk to any modelers who really run their locomotives a lot; the more the locomotives run, the smoother they run. This is because the mechanism "wears in." While you will most likely never wear out a locomotive, a small amount of wear will improve performance. When the sharp edges of new gears and any tightness in the shafts have worn away, you will have a smoother-running unit.

If you really want to go a little off the deep end you can accelerate this wear-in period. A tooth care product called Pearl Drops has a small amount of very fine abrasive in it. By applying a small amount of this product to the gears in the drive train and running the unit for several hours you can take that edge and tightness out of a mechanism.

To wear in your locomotive, you should first disassemble your drive train and wash off all lubricants with warm, soapy water. When it's dry, reassemble everything and use Pearl Drops where you would lubricate the gears with gear lube or grease. *Do not* apply Pearl Drops to the motor or wheel bearings. Leave these alone. Now run your unit. If you have a loop of track or can run continuously on your layout, let the unit run for several hours in each direction. A medium speed is fine. After several hours you may need to add more Pearl Drops. When you feel the locomotive has had enough wearing in, tear down the drive train and wash away all traces of the abrasive. Let the parts dry, then reassemble everything and lubricate as you would any other unit.

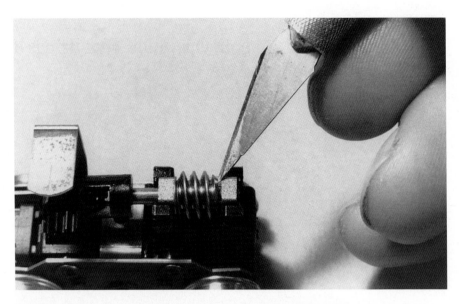

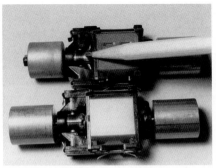

Fig. 2-18. Open-frame motors can suffer from degraded performance if their commutators have a significant buildup of carbon. The bottom motor has a clean commutator, while the commutator of the top motor (at the tip of the pencil) has a deposit that can start to cause problems.

Fig. 2-17. A significant gap between the worm gear and the bearings can result in operational problems, as explained in the text. These washers will remove this free play and cure the problem.

Fig. 2-19. Remove the brushes on an Athearn motor by removing the brush-retaining clip. Do this slowly, since the brush is held to the commutator by a spring.

outward. Do this until the yoke touches the ball only lightly and pivots easily.

Now move to the truck area and inspect all the gears. Check the gears for flash in the teeth or along the edge of the center mounting hole (fig. 2-16). Next, place the drive gears on the appropriate truck pins and turn them by hand. If you note any binds or hear any clicks, check for flash or for problems with the mounting shafts. Next, assemble the trucks except for the worm assembly and push them along a flat surface to check for any binding. If you find no problems, reassemble your chassis and run the unit. If you find any binding now, the problem may be in the worm assembly.

In some cases the fit of the worm gear cover can be a little tight and cause the worm gear to bind against the top drive gear. Trim a little material from the top edges of the worm cover where it is held by the cover locking tabs. This will give the worm gear a little extra room to move and relieve the bind. Only do this if you suspect a bind in this area. Allowing the worm too much unnecessary room will cause more slack in the

drive train, since the worm teeth will not fully mesh with the teeth of the drive gear.

Another potential problem lurks in the worm gear area. Under certain conditions locomotives may lurch or buck. If this condition exists, it will most likely appear on a downhill grade when the cars behind the locomotive roll freely and begin to push against the locomotive. At a certain point at which the locomotive is sort of coasting, or in transition (neither pulling nor being pushed), it may buck. The source of this problem is probably a small gap between the ends of the worm gear and the bearings, as shown in fig. 2-17. The trick is to have only a couple of thousands of an inch of play—the thickness of a sheet of typing paper—between the bearings and the worm gear. While this problem is most common in Athearn units, it can occur in any unit where there is enough slack. Whether you have noted this problem or are getting a new unit ready for the layout and want to prevent it, the solution is to use washers or shims to remove the slack. If you cannot find the thin washers you need, make them from thin sheets of brass. When

dealing with this problem, be careful not to shim too much, causing the worm gear to bind. When you are satisfied with the unit's performance you can lubricate it as discussed earlier in the chapter and put it to work.

The type of motor that powers a unit can also affect its performance. While the can-type motors found in more expensive units are virtually maintenance-free except for lubrication, an open-frame motor will most likely need occasional attention. An open-frame motor is identified by exposed brushes. Athearn units are powered with this type of motor; this is the main difference between them and the more expensive locomotives.

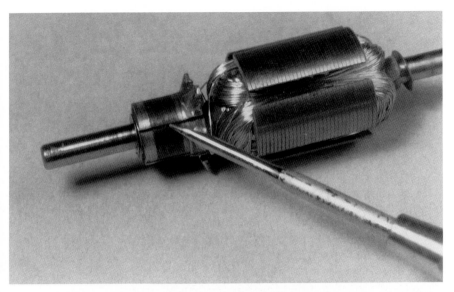

Fig. 2-20. Clean out the gap between the commutator plates as well, since the carbon deposits may conduct small amounts of current between the plates and degrade performance. The tip of a no. 11 X-acto blade will remove the deposits.

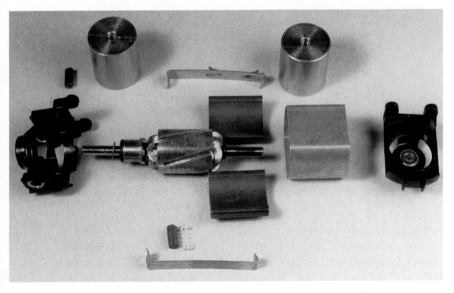

Fig. 2-21. If an open-frame motor appears extremely dirty, you can disassemble it and clean it. Brush rubbing alcohol on the parts to remove accumulated oil and dirt. This is an Athearn open-frame motor.

A telltale sign that an open-frame motor needs attention is a gradual decline in performance. A very visible indication that it needs attention is a heavy black buildup on the motor's commutator. Figure 2-18 shows two Athearn motors. The one above has a bright, brassy commutator, while the one below has a motor that needs attention. These deposits are primarily caused by oil that finds its way onto the commutator and is burnt as it passes between the brushes and the commutator. The oil also causes sparking and excess heat, which may also pit the commutator. You'll have to remove these deposits to restore the motor to proper operation. This is another problem caused by excess lubricant.

It is quite simple to remove the deposits and pits from a motor. Begin by removing the motor from the chassis. Next, remove the brush retainer clip as shown in fig. 2-19. Be careful here—there is a small spring beneath the clip that holds the brush to the commutator. Replace the clips after removing the brushes. Remove one of the flywheels by twisting it off and chuck the motor shaft into a variable-speed drill. Gently secure the motor frame in a vise or find some other way to hold it stationary. I use a fingernail file that has four progressively finer surfaces. You could use emery cloth. Use 600 grit to remove deposits and pits, then switch to 1000 grit to polish the commutator. Run the drill at a slow to medium speed and polish the commutator. Be very careful not to break the armature wires where they are attached to the commutator. Work to progressively finer grades. The final finish should be almost mirrorlike. The smoother the commutator, the better. It should only take a minute or two to do this. When you have finished, use the tip of a no. 11 X-acto blade to remove any material in the gap between the two halves of the commutator (fig. 2-20). Now reassemble your motor and give it a test run.

If excess oil is visible in the commutator or armature area, remove it; otherwise, the problem will recur in short order. To remove the oil properly, remove the armature from the motor frame. To accomplish this, you have to remove both flywheels. Twist the first one off the shaft, then clamp the shaft in a vise and twist off the other flywheel. After you have removed the brush clips, you'll be able to pull off the motor frame ends. Pull the armature from the motor housing while holding the magnets in place. Figure 2-21 shows an Athearn motor totally disassembled. Remove the excess oil by brushing denatured alcohol on the commutator area. Also brush alcohol on the brush-holding end of the motor frame and the

Fig. 2-22. Lower-priced units can have an enclosed truck drive, such as the one shown. These drives can also be disassembled to get to components in need of cleaning.

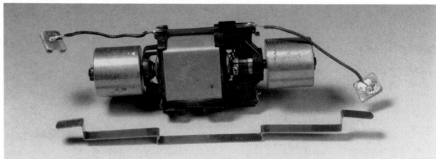

Fig. 2-23. A new wiring harness to replace the Athearn spring clip will result in more reliable electrical contact.

Fig. 2-24. New nickel-silver plated wheels replacing Athearn sintered iron wheels. The new wheels will not oxidize or pick up dirt as quickly as the old ones.

brushes themselves. After the alcohol has evaporated, chuck the commutator end of the shaft in a variable-speed drill and polish the commutator as described previously. When you have finished, reassemble the motor and give it a test run. It should run better than new.

I have treated quite a few Athearn units in this way and have always been pleased with the results. While the technique is most beneficial to older or used units, it may serve as a preventive measure to reduce or delay the formation of deposits on new motors.

You can also use this method to improve performance on lower-priced locomotives. Many lower-priced locomotives are powered by truck-mounted motors (fig. 2-22). Although they are not as durable and reliable as the drives on more expensive units, you can tune up these self-contained units for more reliable operation.

Since these drives come in several different designs, you must figure out how to gain access to the brushes and armature to perform the tuneup.

Another problem to look for if the motor suffers from power loss is a broken armature wire. There should be no loose ends in the armature winding. Such a loose end indicates a broken wire. If you find one,

you may be able to fix it with very careful soldering. Solder a short piece of similar wire to the broken ends and secure the patch back to the armature with some Walthers Goo. If you cannot fix the wire, you must either replace the motor or be content with less power.

UPGRADING DIESEL LOCOMOTIVE COMPONENTS

You can improve performance of the basic Athearn locomotive by replacing several parts. The first and easiest to replace is the motor connector clip. The Athearn part is just a thin piece of spring steel that provides an electrical path between the motor and the trucks. While it is gen-

erally reliable, it does have to be bent correctly so that it maintains continuous electrical contact. A better method involves a simple wire harness. This is nothing more than a piece of braided insulated wire that is soldered to the motor brush clip and has simple electrical connectors on the ends. One could solder the ends of the wire directly to the trucks, but the wires would have to be unsoldered every time the trucks had to be removed. Figure 2-23 shows a simple harness made to replace the original part.

Replace the wheels. The wheels are another area that is quite easy to improve. The Athearn sintered-iron wheels are perfectly functional and

Fig. 2-25. Clean traction tires on a regular basis, since dirt can build up on and under them. Replace them if they become hard or develop flat spots.

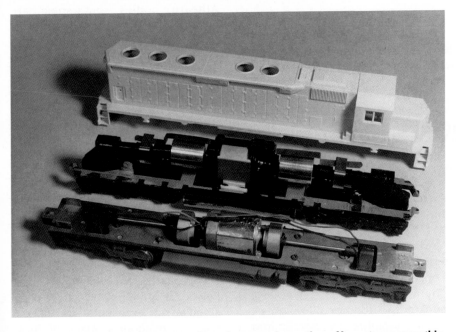

Fig. 2-26. A modeler usually has a variety of repowering options. You can repower this Rail Power SD45 body by using a modified Athearn SD45 chassis or an Overland SD45 chassis, which will fit the body without modification.

will give many years of service, but their surface is somewhat rough. The rough surface allows dirt to stick a little more easily, making more cleanings necessary. Two companies that make replacement wheels are Jay-Bee and NorthWest Short Line. They offer solid nickel-silver wheel sets to fit the Athearn power truck.

Replacing the wheel sets is easy. Just remove the bottom gear box clip from the locomotive, and you can lift out the wheel sets. Twist out the old wheels, being careful not to loosen the axle bearings. Slip the axle bearing on the new axle and push it into place. Take care to push the axle straight into the plastic center drive gear so it does not split. Also, be sure the plastic drive gear is centered between the new wheels. Figure 2-24 shows this procedure. Use an NMRA gauge to check the wheel gauge. The wheel flanges should fit perfectly in the gauge. If they don't, adjust them until they are. One final step before reassembly is to roll the wheels on a flat surface. This is to check for wobbling. If you find any, give the offending wheel a partial turn and check again. The new wheels will not be the problem, since the axle is perfectly square with the wheel, but the plastic center may be slightly sprung. A slight turn may seat the axle squarely. Check again. When you're satisfied, replace the wheels and put the cover on again. The new wheels, being smoother, may slightly decrease the pulling power of your locomotive, but that smooth surface will not pick up dirt as easily and will require less cleaning. Better contact means better operation.

Refit the traction tires. While on the subject of wheels, I should mention the "traction tires" found on some lower-priced locomotives. These tires are like small rubber bands or O rings that fit into a groove in the wheel. Their purpose is to increase traction in lighter, underpowered locomotives. The problem with such a system is that it reduces the number of wheels that pick up electric current, which can cause contact problems. Another problem is that over time they can harden and not contribute much to the locomotive tractive effort they were intended to improve. If you leave them sitting on the track for long periods of time without running, they can also develop flat spots that will cause a noticeable bump when run.

You can do several things to improve the operation of these locomotives. First, keep the wheels clean, because only half of the locomotive wheels are picking up power. Keep the traction tires in place. Removing them will leave a gap in the wheel that will cause all sorts of operational problems. If the tires become hard or develop flat spots, replace them. Remove the wheel from the truck and, using very fine tweezers or a sharp object, lift up the traction tire

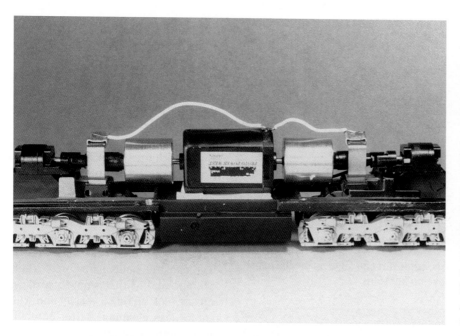

Fig. 2-27. An Athearn SD9 chassis that has been remotored with an A-Line kit. Adding a quality can motor to Athearn units will give them top-of-the-line performance.

and remove it (fig. 2-25). Replace it with a new tire.

These locomotives equipped with traction tires are not the most reliable, but with some care they can be made to operate decently.

Replace the chassis. If you want top performance from your Athearn, Bachmann, or similar units comparable to that of Atlas and Kato units, you can resort to a more drastic upgrade. You can replace the entire chassis. Two companies offer complete chassis for an extensive line of body shells. Proto Power West offers tuned, remotored Athearn chassis. Not only do they fit their intended Athearn bodies, but some are custom milled to fit a number of other manufacturers' shells. With their new motor, additional weight, and tuned drive train, these chassis will run as well as any of the more expensive units, proving that the basic Athearn drive train is as good as any. The only thing the modeler must do is figure out some way to mount the Proto Power chassis to any non-Athearn shell.

Overland, the brass import company, also offers an extensive line of chassis to fit a variety of shells, including many of the Rail Power bodies. Figure 2-26 shows an Overland chassis that will fit the Rail Power SD45 body shell. These chassis also run excellently and have a few added goodies. Many of these chassis have sprung axles, a great feature that will allow the truck to negotiate irregularities while allowing the wheels to remain in perfect contact. Another benefit is that the drive train has an extremely low profile. The truck gear towers are very low, allowing a modeler to add a complete cab interior to the body shell and not interfere with the truck motion. Still another benefit, at least for Rail Power shells, is that the coupler pads are designed so that the Kadee coupler boxes hold the shell in place when installed through the pilot opening.

N SCALE DIESEL LOCOMOTIVES

N scale has benefited in recent years by the introduction of a number of top-notch diesel locomotives. Here again Kato and Atlas have led the way. Quite a few locomotives are offered by other companies as well, and while they all run quite well, they are not up to Kato and Atlas standards in performance.

In most respects N scale is similar to HO and larger scales. The parts are basically the same, only smaller. The same guidelines apply regarding adjustment and lubrication. The real difference is that not many parts and options are available to the modeler who wants to upgrade the performance of a unit. Replacement motors for each manufacturer's units are usually what is available. The can-type motors so prevalent in larger scales are not as common in the small N scale sizes. The easiest units to modify are car-body-type units like the EMD E and F

units. A decent new motor could be fit into this space. The narrow road-switcher units give the modeler less than ½" to work with—not much room to do anything.

An added problem for a remotor project in N scale is that most of the space under the hood not taken up by the motor and drive train is occupied by additional weights—and these weights are often an integral part of the chassis itself. You would probably have to modify these weights if you installed a different motor. You can modify weight with a motor tool. Use the new motor as a guide when removing material. Fit the motor into the modified cavity, install the universal shaft ends, connect the motor terminals, and make sure the motor is properly insulated from the frame. Electrical tape will work well for this. Test-run and make any adjustments until everything works properly.

The only drawback to either of these options is that they are expensive. If you were just to buy a particular locomotive shell and one of these chassis, your cost would be in the price range of a Kato or Atlas unit. There is no free lunch anywhere.

Replace the motor. If you want to save a few bucks, or if you just want to do it yourself, several companies offer replacement motors and complete remotor kits to accomplish the same thing. Alco Products offers drop-in replacement motors for Athearn and several other HO locomotives. All you have to do is pull out the old motor, drop in the new, connect the wires and driveshafts, and turn it loose. A-Line was one of the first to offer motors and repower kits. They have an extensive line of motors, flywheels, weights, and mounting tape. Their kits have good instructions that explain the whole process.

Installing one of these kits in an Athearn chassis is easy. Start by removing the old motor from the chassis. Although it is not part of the kit, A-Line makes a motor-mount cradle weight that drops into the motor cavity. This not only serves as a good base upon which to mount the motor, but adds weight to increase pulling power. Secure the weight to the chassis with epoxy or silicone sealer. The A-line kit includes new flywheels. Use its flywheel cement to secure the new flywheels to the motor shafts; cyanoacrylate will not be strong enough. Use this material sparingly. Do not get any on the motor bearings or there will be major trouble. Trust me—I speak from experience. Solder the wire that leads to the motor terminals before mounting the motor. Test-fit the motor to be sure that it is centered between the truck gear towers, so the driveshafts will reach the flywheels. Secure the motor with either double-faced foam tape or silicone sealer. Attach your wires and driveshafts, and your unit is ready to roll. Test-run the unit. If it runs in reverse

Fig. 2-28. Brush dust and other loose dirt off the unit. Use a soft brush and a light hand.

direction, simply reverse the trucks. Figure 2-27 shows a completed A-Line repowering of an Athearn SD9 chassis.

REPAIRING DIESEL LOCOMOTIVES

Most model locomotive sold today are fine runners. They are well engineered and are built with strong material that with periodic maintenance will run for many years. Yet there are times (although rare) when a unit will break down and need repair. Until recent years locomotive trouble was either a mechanical problem or a simple, straightforward problem with the simple DC electrical system. With the widespread use of DCC and other electronic components, a whole new world of locomotive trouble can now appear.

Electrical repair. If your locomotive is dead and is completely silent when you apply power, the problem is most likely electrical. Obviously, the first thing to check is whether power is reaching the locomotive. Verifying that, you'll have to look inside. Remove the shell and check for loose or broken wires or connections. Leave the chassis on a powered piece of track and move wires and connections—a broken wire or

loose connection may become apparent when it's moved.

Next, remove or bypass any lighting circuits or DCC equipment. If the locomotive runs fine with any of these items removed, you have found your problem. Troubleshooting electronic devices is beyond the scope of this book. Refer any such problems to the manufacturer or someone with knowledge of these items.

If the problem is not electronic or in the wiring, go right to the heart of the matter. Use jumper wires and touch the motor terminals. This will determine if the motor is the problem. If the motor does not run, you have found your problem. The motor is probably shot and should be replaced—there is little that can be repaired on such small motors. If the motor runs, it is simply a matter of finding what is causing the electrical gap and fixing it.

Mechanical repair. Mechanical problems in model locomotives are more likely to result from abuse than use. The drive train of a high-quality locomotive is strong and durable enough to handle most operating conditions. Short of continuous running pulling heavy trains, your locomotives should last many years with only routine maintenance. Careless handling when off the track is the a prime source for trouble. Small children should be supervised when playing with their trains, even if it is their layout. While most model locomotives, especially the tinplate variety, are built to withstand wear and tear, they all should be treated with care. Our locomotives are operating models and in order to operate must be within certain mechanical tolerances. Mishandling and abuse can cause these tolerances to be exceeded, which will cause operational problems.

Bent, broken, misaligned parts or foreign objects will cause operational problems. When a locomotive that has previously run well begins acting up and dirty wheels or lubrication are not the problem, it is time to look deeper. After removing the body shell, look at the visible parts of the drive train for any obvious problems. If you don't see any, run the unit and check for driveshaft or wheel problems. If the problem is still not apparent, remove the trucks from the chassis. Push each truck by hand down a piece of track to check for any binding or wobbling. Run the motor with the driveshafts removed to check for a bent shaft or binding. The key is to isolate the problem. If you find a

damaged part and cannot repair it, replace it with a new one. All makers of high-quality locomotives stock spare parts. Sometimes spare parts are available at your local hobby shop, or a salesperson can order them for you. If not, you can order direct from many manufacturers, some even by phone. There will be a charge for the new parts unless you can prove that the parts were factory-defective. If you are ordering direct, use the parts diagram that came with your locomotive and order by number.

Worn-out locomotives are very rare. Most modelers do not even begin to rack up the mileage necessary to wear out a locomotive. Even if wear does become a factor, the most likely result will be extra slack in the drive train. Only in the most extreme cases will a drive train be worn out to the point of skipping gears. In that likelihood you can try either replacing the worn parts or giving the chassis a well-deserved retirement and buying a new one.

Cosmetic repair. All previous discussion in this chapter has dealt with mechanical and electrical problems. While they are important from an operating standpoint, they contribute little to the external appearance of a locomotive. Maintaining the appearance of a locomotive, whether

it is large scale tinplate or tiny N or Z scale, is not difficult. Dust is easy to remove with a small, soft paintbrush. The soft bristles will not harm even the most delicate parts (fig. 2-28). If a locomotive has stubborn dirt, oil, or grease on the exterior, remove the shell and wash it in warm, soapy water, gently scrubbing it with the same soft brush, and set it aside to dry.

If a locomotive has been handled a lot or abused and paint has been worn or chipped, try to find a matching paint to touch up the damaged areas. If you are unsure about a match, try some in an inconspicuous area or on a separate piece of material. Always wait for the paint to dry before making a final determination—wet paint will seldom dry exactly the same color. With a little weathering the damaged area may be undetectable.

If you can't repair broken parts, you can usually replace them, either through a hobby shop or direct from the manufacturer. You can usually straighten bent parts. Use gentle pressure and try to bend the parts slowly back into shape. A quick jerk can snap off the part completely.

With proper maintenance and care there is no reason why your locomotives should not run as good as new, or even better.

Maintaining & Repairing
Steam Locomotives

CHAPTER THREE

Steam locomotives ruled the rails in this country from the beginning of the railroads until the 1950s. When diesel power became reliable, the steam locomotive was replaced about as fast as manufacturers could build the diesels. Diesel's big advantage was lower maintenance and basic simplicity. In a way, that describes the difference between steam and diesel in the modeling world as well. Just one look at an operating model steam locomotive will reveal the source of the problem. All that beautiful operating machinery is a joy to behold, but it can be a bear to maintain and repair.

BASIC LOCOMOTIVE COMPONENTS AND TERMINOLOGY

The sight of a model steam locomotive rolling slowly down the track with the rods and valve gear turning in perfect synchronization cannot be equaled by anything powered by an internal combustion engine, model or the real thing. Unfortunately, the same thing that makes these machines so interesting and creates the passion for them can also be the cause of significant grief and frustration. The steam modeler must not only deal with the standard electric motor and drive train, which can have many problems of their own, but with a myriad of interconnected

moving parts that make up the running gear. So before beginning any maintenance or repair work on your steam locomotives, you'll want to review the workings of a steamer and the related terminology.

Exterior components. Figure 3-1 shows the major external parts of a typical steam locomotive. Figure 3-2 shows in greater detail the wheel and associated drive components of a typical locomotive.

Electrical components. The electrical pickup and drive mechanism of model steam locomotives is basically the same as that of diesels. The electrical energy is picked up by the drivers, which are electrically isolated

Fig. 3-1. The main external components of a typical steam locomotive

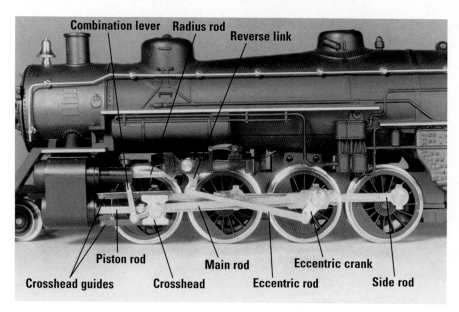

Fig. 3-2. The main drive train components of a typical model steam locomotive

from the other side, just as on diesel locomotives.

Mechanical components. A series of reduction gears transfers the motor torque to the wheels—again, just as in diesel locomotives. In most model steam locomotives there is no need for a driveshaft, so the motor is mounted right on the drive assembly and the worm gear is mounted right on the motor shaft.

Unlike diesel locomotives, whose drive components are internal and whose only animation is the actual turning of the wheels, steam locomotives' drive components are not only visible but in plain sight.

INSPECTING NEW STEAM LOCOMOTIVES

Check the wheel gauge. One of the first things to do with a new unit (and occasionally with older units) is to check the gauge of the wheels. This is easy to do with an NMRA gauge. The wheel flanges should fit perfectly in the gauge slots, and the wheel flange depth should not exceed the depth of the slot.

Adjusting the gauge on the pilot, trailing truck, and tender is easy. First, remove the truck from the unit. The pilot truck wheels are quite accessible because the frame is usually inside the wheels. They can be

adjusted while they're still attached to the truck frame. Grasp the wheels and twist them until one turns on the axle. As they turn, either push them in or pull them out as needed. Check your progress with the gauge and repeat until they're perfect. The trailing truck and tender axles will most likely have to be removed because the truck frame is usually at the ends of the axles. If you spread the frame slightly, you'll be able to lift the axles out or they should fall out on their own. Adjust the wheel spacing the same way as on the front truck axles. After adjusting these axles, secure the wheels with a small drop of cyanoacrylate adhesive for added strength. Place it at the inside of the wheel where the axle passes through.

When reinstalling the trucks or even just checking the gauge, pivot the trucks to the extremes of their motion and check for binding or anything that interferes with their range of movement. Burrs in the mounting holes may cause binding. Use a file to remove them. Adjust or remove anything that interferes with the normal range of motion. There is usually some type of spring in the pilot and trailing truck mounting that gives additional downward pressure to the truck. The trucks are quite light, and without this spring pressure they derail easily. These springs are visible in fig. 1, next to the appropriate trucks. Be sure to put this spring back into place when you remove the trucks. If your lead or trailing truck does derail frequently and the wheel gauge is correct, you may have to increase the spring pressure. Do so by stretching the spring or finding a stiffer spring.

Adjusting the gauge on the main drivers is much more difficult. Not only must you remove the rods from the wheel, but you must not change the position of the crank pin in relation to the crank pin on the opposite driver. The pin on the left side is positioned 90 degrees ahead of the pin on

DISASSEMBLING STEAM LOCOMOTIVES

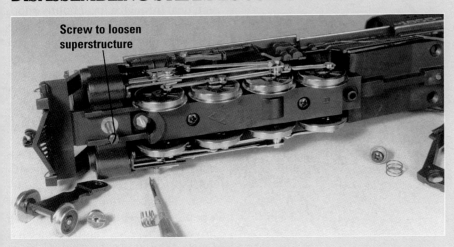

Screw to loosen superstructure

Fig. 1. The underside of a locomotive, showing the location of the screw that holds the running gear to the superstructure. The photo also shows the front and rear trucks removed, as well as the screw and spring that go with each.

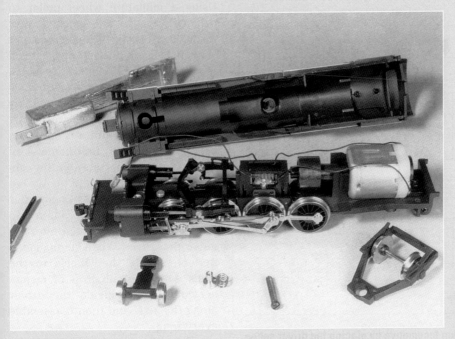

Fig. 2. The superstructure has been removed to expose the motor and drive train components.

Before starting to disassemble or adjust a steam locomotive, follow any specific instructions for disassembly provided by the manufacturer. It makes life much easier if the disassembly procedure is illustrated, or at least explained, especially for the novice. If the manufacturer provides no specific disassembly instructions, examine the exploded view closely; look for any long screw or screws that install from the bottom and will probably reach the superstructure. They are most likely the disassembly screws (fig. 1).

Before starting the disassembly, take a close look at the assembled unit or at what you are going to remove, even if you have good instructions. Too often it is only after everything is apart that we wonder how it looked assembled. A few moments of time spent studying the locomotive can prevent a lot of head-scratching and wondering how it all fits together again later.

While it is not necessary, it is not a bad idea to remove at least the superstructure of your unit when you first get it (fig. 2). If you plan to run the unit at all, you'll have to do the procedure eventually for maintenance, so why not familiarize yourself with it early on? Study the mechanism, put it on the track, and run it to see how everything works. This can be invaluable if problems develop or if the unit will not run at all later. At least you will know how everything should operate. Pay especially close attention to the rods and valve gear movement. This is particularly important for the novice, because the movement of these parts will be a bewildering jumble of motion at first. Study the movement of each part and see how it interacts with other parts. The jumble of motion will resolve itself into a series of simple, coordinated, understandable movements. It is important to have a basic understanding of how the running gear operates in order to troubleshoot any problems that may develop later.

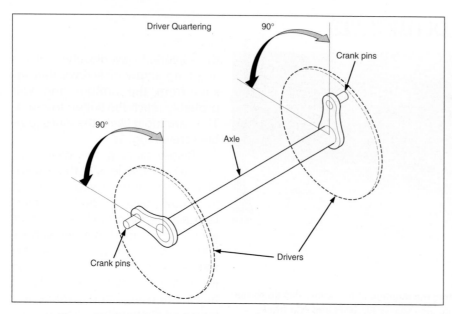

Fig. 3-3. Driver quartering. While it is not necessary that the angle be exactly 90 degrees, it is necessary that all drivers on a locomotive be quartered the same.

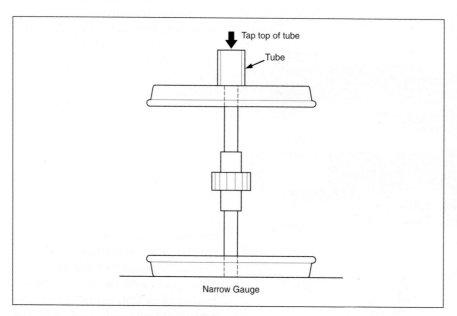

Fig. 3-4. Narrow the wheel gauge on a steam locomotive by placing the driver set on its side, placing a tube slightly larger in diameter than the axle over the center of the top wheel, and tapping gently. Concentrate the force of the tapping as near as possible to the axle to prevent the wheel from breaking.

the right side (fig. 3-3). (This is called "quartering.") It is not so important that the difference be exactly 90 degrees but that all sets of drivers have exactly the same degree of quartering. Simply put, you cannot twist the driver on the axle to adjust the gauge, as you can on the truck and tender axles. You can only push or pull the driver longitudinally along the axle. Any twisting of the axle will change the quartering so that when you replace the axle and hook up the rods, the drive mechanism will bind.

If you have a brand-new unit whose main drivers are out of gauge, you may want to return the unit. If you deal through a local hobby shop, you can explain the problem; maybe they will adjust it for you or allow you to select another unit. Bring your gauge along to show them the problem. If they allow you to exchange the unit, check the new unit for correct gauge. This is one advantage of dealing with a local shop.

If you must adjust the gauge yourself, it is not that difficult, provided that you follow a few guidelines. The first thing to remember when dealing with steam locomotive drivers is that they can be somewhat fragile. Most, if not all, plastic locomotive drivers have a metal "tire" around the outside for electrical pickup. The inside or spoked portion is plastic. Using a miniature wheel puller to adjust the gauge will almost always result in breaking the plastic center section. Even on brass or metal steam locomotives whose drivers are metal, a puller may break the spokes.

To narrow the wheel gauge, lay the driver flat on its side. Use a short section of tubing with a center hole slightly larger than the diameter of the axle. Place the tube on the center hub of the driver and gently tap the driver down (fig 3-4). Check your progress often so you do not go too far. It shouldn't take much effort to move the driver. When the gauge is perfect, secure the wheels to the axles with a small drop of cyanoacrylate placed inside the driver along the axle, and then reassemble everything.

To widen the gauge you must support the inside of the driver as closely to the hub as possible. This can be accomplished in two ways: by cutting a slot in a piece of metal or wood that will support the inside of the driver, or by laying two pieces of metal across two blocks and sliding the metal pieces as close to the hub as possible on each side of the axle. When the hub is supported adequately, use a center punch or piece of metal rod slightly smaller in diame-

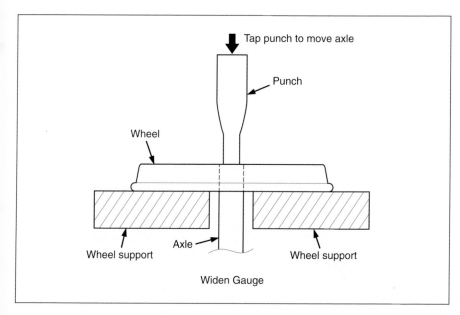

Fig. 3-5. Widen the wheel gauge by sliding the wheel set into a slotted plate to support the wheel. Position a small punch on the end of the axle and give it some gentle taps, just enough to move the axle. The slot should be only slightly larger than the axle diameter to support the wheel as much as possible.

Fig. 3-6. There is often room to mount an operating coupler behind the pilot.

Fig. 3-7. How to install a Kadee coupler behind the front pilot. There isn't room for the coupler box, so screw the coupler directly to the bottom of the pilot. Leave the screw slightly loose, so the coupler can swivel from side to side. While this is not an ideal situation, it does allow an operating coupler to replace the unusable dummy coupler.

ter than the axle and tap gently on the axle to push it downward (fig. 3-5). Again, check your progress often, and when the gauge is perfect, secure with cyanoacrylate and reinstall.

It is important not to put unnecessary pressure on the outside edges of the drivers at any time. This could result in bending the spokes, causing a wobble in the wheel that would be difficult or impossible to remove. Prevention is easier than fixing.

Check the couplers. The couplers you use on your locomotives are a matter of personal choice. Obviously, if you already have an operating layout, you will add the same type of coupler as you use on the rest of the layout. In N scale the choice is between the Rapido coupler and the Micro-Trains knuckle-type coupler. In HO it is between the X2F (horn-hook) and a knuckle type made by a number of manufacturers. In larger scales the choice is similar.

Before deciding what type of coupler to use, you should decide whether you will install an operating coupler on the front of the unit. Some units are equipped with a dummy coupler on the front because the cowcatcher does not allow enough room for an operating coupler. If you plan to operate your unit in only one direction, you can leave the dummy coupler as is. If you want the flexibility of switching with both ends of the unit you'll have to add a coupler to the front. There is often room behind the cowcatcher to install a coupler box (fig. 3-6). Open the front pilot and install whatever type of coupler you use (fig. 3-7). If the pilot or cowcatcher interferes with operation, you'll have to install a long-shank coupler to reach past the pilot.

If you use the rear coupler that came with your unit, all you have to do is check for proper height and operation. If you must change coupler styles, start by removing the old coupler. On some locomotives you may be able to install the new coupler in the existing coupler box. If that is the case, all you have to do then is check for proper height. If you cannot use the existing box, you'll have to remove it and add a suitable mounting pad for the new coupler. Use the examples in the coupler section of the previous chapter and do the same to your tender and front pilot.

MAINTAINING STEAM LOCOMOTIVES

Maintaining an operating model steam locomotive is basically the same as maintaining a diesel locomotive. The first step in maintaining your locomotive is to familiarize yourself with the exterior and mechanical workings of your model. Most, if not all, high-quality locomotives come with some sort of instructions or parts list with an exploded view of the locomotive.

Basic maintenance is simple. Assuming the locomotive is running well, about all you have to do is clean the wheels when necessary, lubricate the mechanism properly when necessary, and check wheel gauge and truck movement occasionally.

Keep the wheels clean. Wheel cleaning will probably be the maintenance task you perform most often. I explained the wheel-cleaning procedure I prefer in the previous chapter. This method work well on diesels but is even better for steamers because it keeps handling to a minimum. Soak one small end of a paper towel with WD-40. Lay the paper towel over the rails with the WD-40 end closest to the locomotive. If the locomotive and tender unhook easily, separate the two for ease of handling. Run the locomotive onto the paper towel and pull it off by hand, all the while keeping the locomotive running. Release the locomotive again and repeat the process a number of times. If locomotive and tender have not been separated, run the locomotive fast enough that the tender is pulled onto the towel too. These wheels also need cleaning because they pick up current for the rear backup light. Move the towel slightly if the dirt becomes too heavy in one spot. Repeat this cycle until no more dirt appears on the towel. Now move the towel so the locomotive runs onto a dry section a number of times to dry any remaining WD-40.

Most steam locomotives have some type of metal wipers to transfer the current from the wheels to the motor leads. The wipers are located behind the drivers and rub along the back side of the drivers (fig. 3-8). If your locomotive has them, check for dirt buildup on the back side of the drivers where the wipers rub. Also check the wiping surface itself, as dirt will accumulate at this point. Without periodic cleaning the dirt will build up to the point at which the wiper can no longer maintain continuous contact. The tip of a no. 11 X-acto blade works well for removing any accumulation of dirt. Scrape the wiper contact point a little with the

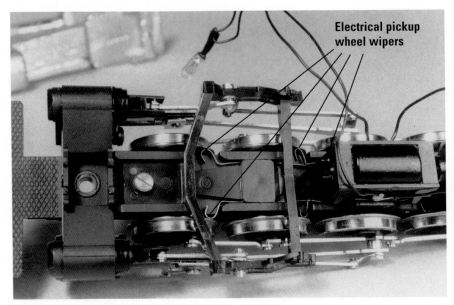

Electrical pickup wheel wipers

Fig. 3-8. This photo shows the wheel wipers and how they make contact with the backs of the wheels.

knife to remove any oxidation that may have formed. Be careful not to bend the wipers too far back when cleaning them. The wiper arms need adequate spring pressure to maintain proper contact. Remove dirt buildup on the back of the wheels by dipping a Q-tip in some Goo Gone or WD-40 and wiping off the crud. The entire back of the wheel surface will probably not be accessible at one time, so turn the wheels as necessary until everything is clean.

Cleaning your locomotive wheels, especially if they are quite dirty, should improve performance significantly. If your locomotive does not respond to cleaning or if operation is still erratic, you will have to look deeper. Refer to the section later in this chapter on troubleshooting and possible remedial action to correct problems.

Lubricate mechanical components. As I explained thoroughly in the previous chapter dealing with diesel locomotives, the need for lubrication is a function of use or lack of use. Obviously, an extensively run locomotive will need lubrication more often. The key word here is more *often,* not more lubricant. Never over-

lubricate any locomotive. Excess lubricant doesn't stay where you put it. It ends up where it is not needed and attracts dirt. Once dirt begins to build up it acts as a wick and attracts more oil, which attracts more dirt. . . . You get the picture. Eventually you have a gummed-up mess in and around the drive train, which you'll have to remove. Preventing this mess is much easier than cleaning it up.

To lubricate a steam locomotive properly, you must usually remove the superstructure. You may be able to reach all the necessary bearings of some locomotives without removing the superstructure, but they are the exception.

What lubricants to use? That is up to you. If you have a particular brand that gives you the desired results, keep using it. My own personal preference is the Labelle line of lubricants. They have an extensive variety of lubricants to suit most needs. To lubricate motor bearings and all other metal-to-metal bearings I use Labelle's 108 Plastic Compatible Motor Oil. Figure 3-9 shows the typical lubrication points. Even if you are lubricating a brass locomotive, it is a good idea to use a plastic-compatible

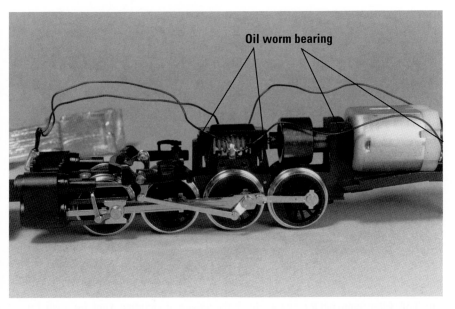

Oil worm bearing

Fig. 3-9. Lubricate the motor and worm gear with a plastic-compatible oil. Lubricate the worm gear and the drive gears with a light grease.

oil because there probably are plastic bushings and other such parts in the drive train. The plastic-compatible oil also will not damage paint. Take care, however, not to get oil on a visible painted surface—it will darken and possibly stain a flat finished surface. Use a small amount of oil on each bearing, only enough to cover the shaft and bearing surfaces. In fact, after adding lubricant it is a good idea to use a corner of a tissue to wick up excess oil.

Lubricate the gear train with either Labelle 102 Plastic Compatible Gear Lube or 106 Plastic Compatible Grease with Teflon. The gear lube and grease are heavier products that will not be thrown off the spinning drive train gears. They stay where they are put. To lubricate the gears, you must remove the bottom axle retainer plate. Have your locomotive upside down for this; otherwise, the driver axles will fall out. After removing the plate, check the amount of lubricant or crud inside the gearbox. If there is any buildup of grease or dirt, try to wipe it out. Use a Q-tip or even a toothpick to scrape out as much of the material as possible. Do not attempt to reuse any of the material

by spreading it on the gears, because this is probably a mix of dirt and lubricant. This goo is the equivalent of oil-soaked mud, not something that should be used on a fine mechanism. After removing as much of the old lubricant as possible, add a little gear lubricant or grease to the tops of the gears and also a little dab to the worm gear; then close the cover. The lubricant will spread evenly over the gears when the locomotive is run.

A note here about new locomotives. Just because a locomotive is new does not mean it is properly lubricated. If the locomotive has sat on the shelf for a long time, the solvents in the lubricant may have evaporated, leaving a heavy residue. Even if your unit is factory-fresh, don't count on proper lubrication. It is very unlikely that your unit did not receive enough lubricant; more likely, it was overlubricated, maybe even excessively. This excess lubricant should be removed, or it will become a dirt magnet. Remove the superstructure and wipe off as much excess lubricant as possible. Open up the gear case and do the same inside it. Now apply the proper lubricant to the appropriate places.

If a locomotive has sat for a long time without running, most of the solvents in the lubricant might have evaporated, leaving a heavy residue of dirt and old lubricant. The residue might have even hardened into a crusty deposit. If you try to run the locomotive first, this problem will manifest itself as slow, sluggish operation. While the sluggish operation may not seem like a significant problem, it will result in a much higher current draw on the motor. In extreme cases, this can damage or even burn out the motor. Before adding more lubricant, try to remove any residue from the bearing and gear areas. Now apply the proper lubricant and your unit should operate just fine.

There may come a time when the built-up crud inside the gearbox and on the drive train parts becomes an operational problem. Then it may be best to tear down the drive train and wash the parts. Do this to remove excess lubricant when the unit is new, as well. Because the steam locomotive drive train is so interconnected, you must do this procedure with care. Then you won't bend or damage the rods and valve gear mechanism, and you'll be able to get everything back together and operating properly again.

After removing the parts, soak them in a warm-water-and-soap bath. Using an old toothbrush, gently scrub the crud from the parts. When the parts are clean, rinse them in warm water and set them aside to dry. When everything is dry, reassemble the drive train and lubricate everything as previously described.

FINE-TUNING STEAM LOCOMOTIVES

Diesel operators have it easy in comparison to steam locomotive operators. There are not such wide-ranging differences in wheel arrangements, and they don't have to deal with the all the running gear. A simple little 0-4-0 switcher can give you a lot of grief. Just imagine dealing with a

4-8-4 or, even worse, an articulated locomotive with a 4-8-8-4 nightmare of a wheel arrangement! You've really gotta love steam to put up with the abuse the drive train can provide.

The terms tuneup and repair are fairly self-explanatory, but where tuneup ends and repair begins is rather vague. To keep things as simple as possible on this complex subject, this section will deal with each major area of the drive mechanism and attempt to diagnose and solve the problems associated with each.

Diagnosing problems. Your scale steam locomotive is a complex piece of equipment. When problems develop, finding the source of the problem can often be more difficult than solving it. The following troubleshooting guide will be general in nature, although I'll cover some topics thoroughly. It is impossible to list all possible problems or combinations of circumstances that cause them and the corrective action needed to fix them. When you're troubleshooting problems, the idea is to become more analytical. You want to analyze the locomotive by sections to isolate a problem, not look at the whole locomotive at one time and become overwhelmed.

The first order of business is to make sure you have performed all of the normal maintenance tasks. Have you cleaned the wheels? Have you cleaned the electrical contacts, and are they in contact? Have you lubricated the mechanism properly? If the unit is still not running properly, then it is time to look deeper.

What if your unit does not run at all, not even a hum or a glowing light? It is most likely an electrical problem. Remove the superstructure and check for obvious problems: broken wires, loose connections, anything out of the ordinary. If you find nothing, try hooking up the power pack leads directly to the motor terminals. If your motor runs, the problem is somewhere between the motor and the wheels. To isolate the problem,

Check universal couplings

Fig. 3-10. After removing the motor, check the universal coupling. Look for flash, foreign material, or broken parts that will cause problems.

set the unit on a section of track with the power on. Use a jumper wire from one rail to its corresponding motor terminal to determine which side of the unit's electrical path is causing the problem. Once you expose the culprit "dead" side, use the jumper wire to determine which section has the broken connection. It is just a matter of using a little detective work to find the problem and repair it.

If the motor does not run with the power pack leads hooked directly to it, it definitely needs attention. First, turn the motor shaft to see if it is loose and turns easily. If the motor begins to run when turned, the problem may be dirt under one of the brushes or a heavy buildup of carbon on the commutator. Carbon buildup on the commutator is a common problem on open-frame motors. Remove the carbon buildup using a very fine sheet of Flex-i-grit or similar material. It will be easier to work on the motor if you remove the motor from the chassis. If you can remove the brushes, so much the better, but be careful not to lose the brush springs when removing the brushes. An in-depth explanation of this procedure appears in the previous chapter on diesel locomotives. After you

remove the carbon and polish the commutator, your motor should run like new again.

If the motor turns hard or not at all, the bearings are tight or there may be some foreign material caught between the armature and the magnets. Apply a little penetrating oil or WD-40 to the motor bearings. If the bearings are tight, this may loosen them. If the motor now turns more easily, try running it again. If the bearings are the problem, running the motor with WD-40 applied to the bearings should loosen them up. When the motor turns freely again, apply a small drop of Labelle 108 to small scale motors or 107 to larger scale motors.

If the bearings are not the problem, then there may be something between the armature and the magnets. Remove the motor from the chassis and see if you can find the problem. You may dislodge the offending material just by turning the motor shaft. If not, try to disassemble the motor frame to get at the problem. An open-frame motor can be disassembled, but the enclosed case of a can motor should be left alone unless you are experienced in working with these motors (even though

Fig. 3-11. If you suspect a problem in the running gear of a locomotive and you cannot locate it, it may help to remove the worm gear and push the locomotive by hand. You may be able to feel or see the problem.

it's possible to take them apart). Besides, the tightly enclosed case of a can motor makes it highly unlikely that any foreign material has found its way inside. If you can get the motor apart, wipe off the magnets and motor armature with a dry cloth and reassemble. If the shaft spins more freely, try running the motor to see if there is improvement. If there is still a catch in the motor when the shaft is turned, the shaft may be bent. If that is the case, replace the motor. I'll cover that topic later in the chapter.

If your motor still has no life after you've checked the commutator, brushes, and bearings and checked for foreign material, there may be a broken wire internally or some other fatal problem. To try to repair a motor past this point is beyond the scope of this book. Would it even be worth the effort? In some of the lower-cost locomotives a new motor would not be that expensive. In fact, if you want to improve a lower-priced locomotive, you could install a high-quality can motor. I'll cover remotoring a locomotive later.

If the motor checks out okay and your unit still does not move or run properly, it is time to look at the drive

train. The first thing to check is the driveshaft. Many steam locomotives just have a universal connection from the motor to the drive train. Check it for proper operation. If there is a bind here, check for flash or a broken universal "finger" (fig. 3-10). If there is a driveshaft, check the universals at both ends. Some steam locomotive driveshafts are a short section of flexible tubing. In time this tubing can harden and prevent the mechanism from turning easily. You can replace the old tubing with a similar-size piece of new tubing or install a regular driveshaft. NorthWest Short Line has a wide variety of driveshaft components to fit a number of shaft sizes. There is not room in this book to cover all the possibilities dealing with this type of conversion. If the driveshaft or coupling checks out okay, try to turn the driveshaft manually. If the shaft is tight and will not move either way, or if it does move but is very tight, something is broken or lodged in the gear train, valve, or running gear. Remove the motor and worm gear and push the locomotive manually on a piece of track (fig. 3-11). You may be able to see or feel where the problem is. If you feel a

bind or a catch when you push the locomotive, stop when the bind is at its worst and use tweezers to check which running gear components are tight (fig. 3-12). Check the side and main rods for tightness. While the rods should not be so loose that they are sloppy, they should have some slack at all points to allow for side play in the wheels and slack in the gear train. Use tweezers to wiggle the side rods at each driver attachment point. There should be some slack at each point. Next, remove the main rods (fig. 3-13). The eccentric rod and valve gear are also attached to the main rod, so remove them as well. If the problem disappears, your main rods or valve gear are the culprit. Reinstall the rod to one side, then the other to see if one or both are binding. Check the crosshead for tightness or binding. Slide the crosshead in the crosshead guides as shown in fig. 3-14.

If the external running gear check out fine, the problem is in the drive train. Solving this problem is a matter of going through the components one by one to find the trouble. Start at the driveshaft and work toward the worm gear and then into the gearbox. Remove the worm gear to see if the drive gears turn freely without it. If the problem is not here, remove the gearbox cover to get at the drive gears (fig. 3-15). You are looking for damaged, bent, or broken parts or foreign material that may be the cause of the problem. If the problem is not apparent, wash all the components, removing the dirt and lubricant to get a clearer view of things. Inspect parts for wear, broken gear teeth, bent shafts, and the like. If success still eludes you, reassemble the drive train one part at a time and turn them as you add them. The culprit will eventually be apparent.

Troubleshooting and adjustment in this area can try the patience and fray the nerves. If you cannot solve the problem, and if operation of the locomotive is more important than the valve gear, you can remove much or all of it and run the locomotive with the main rod connected to the crosshead. You'll lose some visual interest, but at least the locomotive will run decently.

If you find broken or damaged parts, you may have to replace them. If the unit came with a parts list and you saved it as you should have, you can identify the part. See if your local hobby shop can get a replacement or order one directly from the manufacturer. Many manufacturers have a customer service number. Call and identify your unit and have the part number handy. You will be given prices and payment instructions. If you pay by credit card, the part can often be in your hands in only a few days.

Replace the motor. Obviously, every link in the drive train is important. One poor-quality, bent, or broken component can cause the entire unit to quit or run poorly. But without a good motor the best drive train in the world is wasted. Earlier in this chapter I dealt with some motor tune-up and adjustment procedures, most of which are intended for open-frame motors. There is nothing wrong with a high-quality open-frame motor, but to achieve really top-notch performance a locomotive should be equipped with a quality can motor.

The first step in replacing a motor that is not stock is to determine the space available for the new motor. You can use the old motor as a guide when selecting a replacement; but if extra room is available, why not take advantage of it by installing a larger motor? A larger motor serves several purposes. Obviously, the larger the motor, the more power a locomotive will have. Tractive effort may not be improved, though, unless you add extra weight. A larger motor will handle the extra weight without excess heating. Heat is a mortal enemy of these small motors.

Several manufacturers offer quality can motors in a variety of sizes that will fit a variety of applications from N scale on up. Choose the size

Fig. 3-12. Check for binding or tightness by wiggling individual components with tweezers. There should be some slack in all cosmetic valve components and drive components.

Fig. 3-13. Removing the main rod and valve gear can help locate the source of a difficult problem.

that fits your need. The most important consideration and the key to success in any remotoring project is the ability to connect the motor to the existing drive train. Some locomotive motors have a universal coupling mounted on the shaft, while others have the worm gear itself mounted on the shaft. If the shaft diameter of the new motor is smaller than that of the old, you will need a bushing to mount the universal coupling or worm. If the shaft is larger, you will either have to drill out the parts to fit the shaft or buy new parts that fit the motor shaft. An excellent source of replacement parts is NorthWest Short Line. It offers a very complete line of parts to fit a variety of motors.

Drilling a larger hole in the parts can get dicey—the new hole must be within several thousands of an inch of the shaft size. The hole must also stay centered, since any off-centering will cause a wobble when you add the drive part. Some wobble may be tolerable on a universal coupling, but any such discrepancy on a worm gear will cause binding with the matching toothed gear.

After you have the proper parts to connect your new motor to the drive train, it is time to fit the motor into its new location. If the new motor is similar in size to the old, it may fit with few or no alterations to the old mount. If there is a major difference, you will have to fabricate a

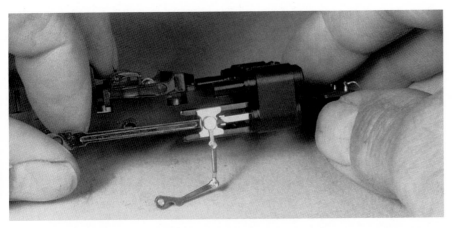

Fig. 3-14. Manually sliding the crosshead back and forth will determine if there is any binding or tightness in the crosshead guides or piston rod.

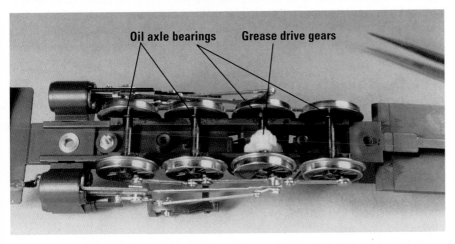

Oil axle bearings   Grease drive gears

Fig. 3-15. The gear box cover has been removed from this IHC steamer, showing the drive gear. The lube points are also visible. Lubricate the axle bearings with a plastic-compatible oil and the drive gear with a light gear grease.

new cradle or mounting base. Fortunately, if you intend to mount the new motor with silicone sealer, which is a preferred method, all you have to do is provide a flat, solid surface on which to rest the motor. The uncured silicone sealer will make its own cradle, which will more than adequately hold the motor when cured. The beauty of using silicone sealer is that after curing it is somewhat flexible, providing the motor with just a little "give." It also helps to insulate the locomotive from any motor vibration.

After you have a suitable motor mount, hold your motor in position and determine at what point on the

motor shaft the worm or universal coupling will have to be located. Mark this position with a marker pen. Securing the coupling or worm is next. If a good tight press fit is possible, that is all you need. If the parts turn easily or are just tad loose, secure them with A-Line Flywheel Cement. This material dries to form a nice tight bond that will not slip on the shaft. Before applying cement to the motor shaft, use a solvent and remove any grease or oil that may be there. Apply a thin coat of the flywheel cement and slide the part into position. Do not get any of this product near the motor bearing. It can be nearly impossible to free a motor shaft after an encounter

with this product. Trust me—I know from experience.

When the cement has dried, apply some silicone sealer to the mounting base, connect the universal couplings or properly position the worm with regard to the worm gear, and nestle the motor into its new home. If the motor will not stay put until the silicone has cured, you must hold it in the proper position in some way until it does so. When the silicone has cured—overnight should be adequate—hook up the motor leads and run the unit to check for alignment problems. Another advantage of using silicone as a motor mount is that it is easy to cut and trim if any adjustment is needed. After making any adjustments, apply a little more sealer and everything will be bonded together again. When everything operates satisfactorily, your remotoring project is complete.

Improve the electrical pickups. The subject of improving electrical pickup depends on whether a problem exists. If a locomotive runs fine and performance suffers only when the wheels become dirty, tinkering with electrical pickup is not necessary. If, however, performance is still somewhat erratic after a good wheel cleaning, maybe a little improvement in this area will help.

If you determine that you need some improvement in pickup, how you proceed will depend on a number of factors. A major consideration is how the electricity is picked up and transmitted to the motor. Can you adjust the existing system to solve the problem? Does the system need assistance or additional pickup capacity to become reliable, or is the system so unreliable or troublesome that it should be scrapped?

There are two basic pickup systems. One relies on wipers that rub against the back of the turning metal wheel or tire. The wipers are hard-wired directly to the motor. The other splits the locomotive in half electrically. Both the frame and the wheels are insulated from the opposite sides, with a motor wire connected to each side.

The wiper system is the simplest, most often found on lower-priced steam locomotives. A thin strip of conductive material is in contact with the back of the metal wheel. Unfortunately the contact points suffer from the same affliction that causes wheel-to-rail problems—dirt and oxidation. The simplest way to improve reliability is to clean the contact points each time you clean the locomotive wheels. I covered this earlier in the chapter, in the section on cleaning wheels. If cleaning the wheels and wipers does not solve the problem, the next step—and also the simplest adjustment—is to check and adjust the wiper pressure on the backs of the wheels. Checking the wiper pressure is easy. Just slip a small screwdriver or knife blade behind the wiper and lift. Too little pressure will allow the smallest piece of dirt to lift the wiper and disrupt the flow of current; too much may cause operational problems by interfering with driver-side play or causing excessive drag on the wheels. While it is possible to measure the actual pressure or force that the wiper applies to the wheel, common sense is all that is necessary to determine proper pressure. If you feel that the wiper pressure is not adequate, the best way to increase pressure is to slide the driver clear of the wiper, note the position of the wiper, and bend it farther out. Do this to the wiper on the other side of the locomotive as well to keep the pressure as equal as possible, especially on the drivers. Uneven pressure on the drivers will affect the driver free play (the sideways movement of the axle that allows the wheel flanges of locomotives with more than two pairs of drivers to ride properly between the rails on curves).

If cleaning and adjusting the wipers don't improve things, it may be time to consider some additional electrical pickup ability. As always, there are several options to consider. One is adding wipers to any drivers

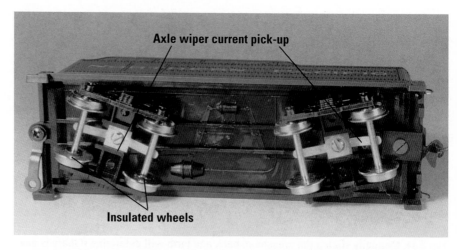

Fig. 3-16. The tender axles have current pickup for the rear light. You could tap this system for additional pickup for the locomotive. If you remove the tender axles for any reason, be sure to return them to the truck in exactly the same orientation. Each axle has one insulated wheel, and these insulated wheels must be properly oriented. One truck's insulated wheels are on one side, and the other truck's are on the other side.

or truck wheels that do not currently have them. The other method is installing pickup shoes that actually slide along the top of the rail.

Adding additional wheel wipers is not difficult. You must find a suitable mounting location and then connect the wiper to the proper electrical terminal. For the wiper itself you can choose a commercially available wiper in a style that best fits the location, or you can make your own from .005 shim brass. Depending on the location in which you intend to mount the wiper, you can either copy an existing wiper on your locomotive or design one to fit the location. Trace the wiper outline with a fine marker pen and cut it out. The thin brass is easy to cut with sharp scissors.

Mount the new wiper with at least one screw to hold it securely to the frame. Drill a hole in the wiper to clear the mounting screw or screws. Now drill the hole or holes in the frame where the wiper will be located. This hole should be tapped, so use the appropriate drill size. Tap the hole and turn the screw into place. Check that the screw does not protrude into any vital area and interfere with locomotive drive parts. If it does, trim the screw appropriately. Solder one end of a short length of

insulated wire to the wiper and the other to the proper electrical terminal. Mount it with the screws and give it the proper bend so it will rub on the wheel properly. Use other wipers as a guide when doing this. To reduce the visibility of this shiny brass, paint it to match the rest of the frame.

The tender axles are another potential source of additional pickup ability. Many tenders have wipers on the axles (fig. 3-16) to pick up current for the rear light. They are already wired for the backup light on the rear, so it would be easy to tap into the existing electrical connections. The only consideration is to have some way of disconnecting the wire leads when you must separate the locomotive and tender. To disconnect the wiring, you could use some type of miniature plug or install a two-wire screw terminal on either the tender or locomotive.

The other option is installing sliding pickup shoes. You will need at least one on each side of the locomotive; two would be better. You can install them anywhere along the bottom of the locomotive. Install them in the same way as the wheel wipers explained a few paragraphs previously. One concern with adding the rail-wiping pickup shoes is the visibil-

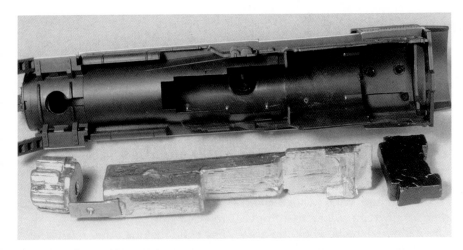

Fig. 3-17. The weights are an important part of a steam locomotive. Be sure to replace them after disassembling the locomotive.

ity of the parts. It is not *that* bad, because the wipers are quite small and the undercarriages of steam locomotives sit fairly low. Some thought to location and a little black paint will make these additions much less noticeable and virtually undetectable from several feet away. Besides, what is more unrealistic and eye-catching—a jerky, erratically running locomotive or several small sliding pickup shoes on a smoothly running unit?

The amount of bend or down-pressure to apply to the pickup shoes is a matter of experimentation. While the shoe has rounded or bent-up ends, there should not be so much pressure that the shoe drops into the flangeways of switch and crossing frogs and snags the trackwork. Just enough pressure to make good contact is all you need.

Adding auxiliary or additional electrical pickup will improve a locomotive's performance. The more paths electricity has to follow, the better likelihood that continuous electrical connection will be maintained. While there is some effort to upgrading the pickup system, the end result will be a more reliable locomotive.

Weight the locomotive. Weight is an important consideration in all locomotives; steam locomotives are no exception. There is usually quite a bit of weight inside a model steamer (fig. 3-17). Whatever boiler or super-structure area is not needed for the drive train is usually filled with weight. It is important to return the weight to the proper position after disassembly. Failure to do so will result in less pulling power or will affect the balance of the locomotive over the drivers and cause additional operational problems.

REPAIRING STEAM LOCOMOTIVES

In external details, steam locomotives are considerably more complex than their diesel counterparts. Essentially, the main body of a steam locomotive is a big boiler with no room for control or auxiliary equipment. Only on some later steamers was there an attempt to streamline or cover some of this equipment. Besides the fascinating exposed running gear, another attraction of steam locomotives is all that exposed detail. While all those goodies are a joy to admire and behold, they can also be a pain to care for. Obviously, the first rule of thumb in caring for any delicate piece of machinery is to keep handling to an absolute minimum. Most if not all damage to locomotives occurs with the wheels off the rails, not on. Large, sometimes clumsy hands can easily bend or break small or delicate details. Even the most experienced modeler can on occasion mishandle a locomotive, resulting in damage. Worse yet are the untrained yet well-intentioned hands of visitors who want to "help" fix a minor problem. Most modelers know how or where to handle their motive power. Those not intimately familiar with the delicate nature of a scale model locomotive do not realize what problems they can cause.

Regardless of how the damage occurred or who did it, the result is that you'll have to fix the damage to maintain the appearance of the locomotive. You must glue back into place any parts that have been broken off. Larger parts will present little problem, but some additional work may be necessary on smaller parts, or parts with a small attachment area, to ensure a strong joint. A relatively easy solution is to reinforce the attachment point by drilling a small hole on each side of the break point and inserting a similar-size piece of wire. Then reassemble the whole thing using cyanoacrylate. The resulting repair will be very strong, maybe even stronger than before breakage. In some cases you may be able to do the same thing without drilling holes. If the back of the part is not visible to someone viewing the locomotive normally, you may be able to reinforce the joint with a piece of styrene, again with wire. Secure the styrene with a solvent-type cement, and secure the wire with a cyanoacrylate adhesive. A thickened cyanoacrylate would be best.

All that piping and those control rods are another potential breakage problem. Many of these components are made of cast or molded plastic; if broken off, they can be nearly impossible to reattach. The best way to repair such damage is to use a similar-diameter brass wire, bend it to match the original, and install the new piece in holes drilled in the appropriate location, securing it with cyanoacrylate. Detail Associates offers a line of brass wire that should meet almost any need. Paint the part to match. Often the repair will be more realistic than the original part it replaced.

What if broken-off parts are lost or are damaged beyond repair? If the

WORKBENCH TIP: Cleaning Your Steam Locomotive

Scale locomotives operate in a less-than-perfect environment. Dust, dirt, oil, and fingerprints are all the result of just being on a layout. Only locomotives tucked away in a box or enclosed display cabinet are immune to these problems. To keep that like-new appearance (or in the case of a weathered unit, that worn and dirty look) you need to do occasional cleaning.

Removing dust is probably the top item on the cleaning list. Use a soft paintbrush and gently dust from the top down. Avoid cheap plastic-bristle brushes—they can actually scratch a delicate weathered surface. To get into tight corners or around complex details, use a smaller brush. If you have an air compressor and an air gun, you can use air pressure to blow the dust out of hard-to-reach places. If you lack an air gun, an airbrush will work fine. Leave off the paint jar and be sure no thinner or cleaner remains in the unit before starting. Just keep the pressure low. Excess pressure can rip off small parts.

There may come a time when dusting is not enough. Oil, grease, fingerprints, smoke residue, and other accumulations will degrade the look of the locomotive. In some cases, such as occasional greasy fingerprints, you can spot-clean an area with a soft cloth dampened with rubbing alcohol or a mild degreasing detergent. Wipe the area carefully, then wipe with a cloth dampened with water to remove any residue. Finally, wipe the area with a dry cloth to remove remaining moisture and prevent spotting.

If that procedure doesn't produce satisfactory results, or if your locomotive needs a more general cleaning, you'll have to wash the locomotive. Start by removing the body from the drive train. Disconnect the rods and valve gear and remove any parts that may be adversely affected by water. If possible, remove any lighting components and weights inside the body. The drive train assembly should be left out of this. Limit any cleaning of the drive train to wiping or spot-cleaning, as described in the previous paragraph.

Clean the body by immersing it completely in a container filled with water and a mild grease-cutting detergent. Use about the same soap concentration as you would to hand-wash dishes. Let the body soak for a while, allowing the water to soften the dirt and oils. Then take a soft brush and gently scrub the model's surface to dislodge the crud. Remove the body and rinse it under hot water. Hot water helps to remove not only the dirt film but any soap residue. After rinsing, it is best to dry the model by patting gently with a soft cloth. Try to blot up all remaining water drops. They may contain residue, or if you have hard water, may leave mineral deposits or water spots. After reassembly your locomotive should look as good as new.

If for some reason you cannot completely immerse your locomotive body in water, you can still wash it. Prepare a container of water and soap mix and use a soft brush dipped in it to gently scrub the external surfaces. Go over the model several times to get off as much dirt as possible. Replace the soapy water with plain hot water and repeat the process to remove all traces of dirt and soap. Now pat dry as previously described and reassemble.

parts are separate detail items, you may be able to get the replacement parts from the manufacturer. If the particular items are not available, your next best option is to try to match the missing or damaged parts to those from commercial parts suppliers such as Precision Scale or Precision Investment Associates. In fact, these parts could be more accurate and detailed than the parts you are replacing. A third option is to cannibalize a damaged or wrecked unit. While chances are slim, you may be able to find such a donor at shows or swap meets for a bargain price. Such a unit is also useful as a source of other parts. You've heard it before and you will hear it again—never throw anything away. You never know when you will need it.

Replacing parts with commercial items is not difficult. Because parts can go in so many different places, it is impossible to cover all potential mounting possibilities. The first step is to study the new part and its intended location to determine the best way to mount it. Next, make any necessary modifications to those areas. If you are mounting parts made from dissimilar materials such as brass and styrene, you will have to use either cyanoacrylate adhesive or five-minute epoxy. Make brass-to-brass joints with solder, cyanoacrylate, or epoxy. Make styrene-to-styrene joints with a liquid solvent. The bottom line in replacing parts is to use common sense and your modeling skills to solve mounting and attachment problems. When you have finished, paint the new parts to match the locomotive.

With some patience and a little skill you can keep your steam locomotive fleet well maintained both mechanically and cosmetically.

Maintaining & Repairing
Rolling Stock
CHAPTER FOUR

Fig. 4-1. Regardless of car type, the basic mechanical components are the same: trucks, couplers, and frame. Only the length of the car and the truck spacing can change.

In terms of mechanical operation, rolling stock or cars are not nearly as complex as powered locomotives, but trouble-free operation is just as important. The most detailed and trouble-free locomotive is wasted if the cars following it are not adjusted and maintained to the same standards. Fortunately, it is quite easy to build, operate, and maintain a top-notch fleet of rolling stock.

All rolling stock, whether it is a freight car, a passenger car, or other equipment, has the same basic foundation. For operational purposes, it is nothing more than a frame to which the trucks and couplers are fastened. Figure 4-1 shows the basic

rolling stock foundation. For modeling purposes, everything else is there for decoration, whether it is a

flatcar or a cylindrical covered hopper. Only the frame length and truck spacing will vary.

BASIC ROLLING STOCK COMPONENTS AND TERMINOLOGY

Before discussing mechanical issues we will deal with proper terminology. Figure 4-2 shows the basic mechanical components of a typical car. Most of these terms are the same in both model and prototype.

INSPECTING NEW ROLLING STOCK

New model rolling stock for the most part comes either ready to run or as easy-to-assemble "shake the box" kits. There are also craftsman-type kits that require significantly more time to assemble. All of these types have the same operational characteristics. Before adding any piece of rolling stock to your layout, check the following things to ensure trouble-free operation.

Check the wheel gauge. The standard tool for checking critical components of rolling stock, like locomotives, is the NMRA gauge for your scale and the NMRA recommended practices (RPs) as your reference source. Begin by using the NMRA gauge to check the wheel gauge. The flanges should fit perfectly on the groves as shown in fig. 4-3. If your wheel flanges are deeper than the gauge grooves, replace the wheelsets or the entire truck. Wheel flanges that are too deep (fig. 4-4) will cause problems at turnouts and crossings by "bottoming out." The bounce caused by bottoming out is both unprototypical and likely to cause derailments. Many of these wheels with deep flanges also have sharp edges, not nicely rounded. These sharp edges may catch on any imperfections in your trackwork and cause additional problems.

Check the wheel tread width as well. Use the wider notch on the NMRA gauge for this (fig. 4-5). The wheel tread should not fit into this notch. If your wheel tread is narrower than the notch, you could be in for problems at crossings and turnouts, since the wheels could drop into the frogs. Such wheels should be re-

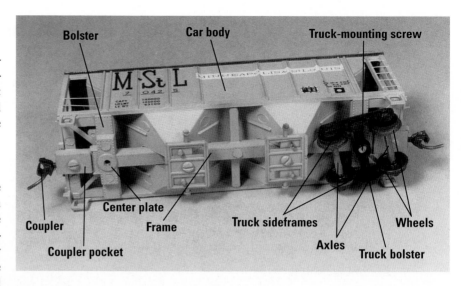

Bolster · **Car body** · **Truck-mounting screw** · **Center plate** · **Coupler** · **Frame** · **Truck sideframes** · **Wheels** · **Coupler pocket** · **Axles** · **Truck bolster**

Fig. 4-2. Basic rolling stock components

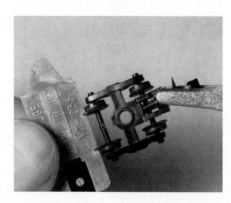

Fig. 4-3. Check the wheel gauge on all rolling stock before the car enters service on your layout.

Fig. 4-4. Check the wheels for proper shape too. The HO scale wheel at the left is the correct shape. Note the rounded edges of the flange. Don't use a wheel like the one at right—the flanges are both too deep and too sharp, not rounded. The deep flange will "bottom out" on switch and crossing frogs, and the sharp edges may catch on track imperfections and derail the car.

placed. There are exceptions to this because there are modelers who use closer-to-scale wheels. This type of modeling is called "fine scale." Even more exacting are the Proto:87 modelers in HO scale and the Proto:48 modelers in O scale who use virtually scale wheels, including flanges. Such groups have slightly different track standards that require closer tolerances for reliable operation of these wheels. Those standards are beyond the scope of this book; so unless you know what you are doing, don't mix fine-scale-equipped rolling stock with regular equipment.

If a wheelset is out of gauge, begin adjustment by removing the wheelset from the truck. Do this by

grasping the wheelset with the thumb and index finger of one hand and pulling back while holding one side of the truck with the same fingers on the other hand. Bending will not hurt the plastic sideframes, as long as you do not overdo it.

The wheels are held in place on the axles by friction. Adjust them by twisting the wheels and either pulling them apart or pushing them together. Grasp the wheels with your thumb and index fingers and twist. The

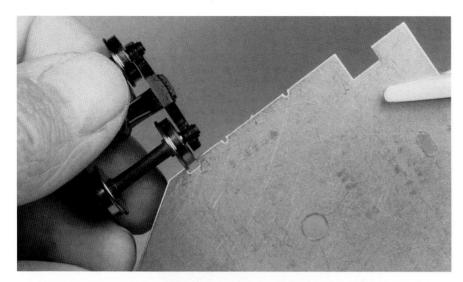

Fig. 4-5. Check the wheel tread for proper width as well, using the NMRA gauge. The wheel tread should not fit into the notch. The wheel shown is correct. Narrow wheel treads can cause problems at frog flangeways.

Fig. 4-6. This snap-in truck on a lower-priced piece of rolling stock does not allow any adjustment.

climb any track irregularity and derail the car. Sometimes new rolling stock has perfectly gauged wheels that are out of center and must be adjusted. To correct centering problems, you need pliers to hold the axle, because you'll probably have to move both wheels. Hold the axle firmly and twist the wheels to the proper location. You may have to check the gauge and centering several times to get it right.

After removing the wheelset from the truck, check the wheel tread and flange for rough spots as well. The flange is the most likely problem area. Turn the wheel while holding it in your fingers to feel for any rough spots. The finger is more sensitive than the eye for this. Remove any burrs or rough spots with fine sandpaper.

When the wheels are properly centered and in gauge, secure the wheels by applying a small drop of cyanoacrylate to the inside of the wheel at the axle. The wheels should fit quite tight on the axles and retain proper adjustment, but a little extra help doesn't hurt.

Check the trucks. For many, simply checking wheel gauge is good enough. But to ensure top-notch operation you should go further and check the entire truck assembly. If you are dealing with a ready-to-run model, remove the trucks. Depending on manufacturer and scale there will be either a screw or some type of friction pin holding the trucks in place. To remove a pin-held truck, slide a small screwdriver between the top of the truck and the bolster and gently pry the truck loose. Remove a screw with the appropriate screwdriver. If you should encounter a truck with the mounting pin cast on the truck frame, as shown in fig. 4-6, replace it for best operation. This is covered later in the chapter.

Most truck sideframes are made of a tough, slightly flexible plastic material that can be slightly adjusted if necessary. First, check for flash or

wheels may be set quite tight on the axles and may take some effort to break loose. Keep the wheels centered on the axle when adjusting the gauge. Usually the small adjustment needed to correct any gauge problem will not be enough to significantly uncenter the wheels, but always give it a look anyway. An "out of tram" truck assembly will cause problems—the wheel flanges will ride the sides of the rail and have a tendency to associated stray pieces of material and remove them, especially around the wheel and mounting pin area. Next, check to make sure the truck frame is not twisted. Look across the tops of the sideframes to make sure they are even. Another way to check this is to place the wheelsets, in the frame, on a piece of track. While you gently place a finger on the center of the bolster, use another finger and press lightly in each sidearm. There should be no rocking, and the axle ends should be in contact with the truck journals. If there is a twist in the truck, remove the wheels and give the frame a good twist in the opposite direction. While the plastic material is tough, a good twist will stretch the plastic slightly and it will take on a new set. Do this until the rocking disappears.

Next, put the wheels back into place. Check for slack or free play between the frame and axles. There should be some slack to allow the wheels to turn freely. Give the wheels a spin, and they should turn freely. If the axle is tight in the journals, bend the ends of the sideframes outward until the axle has some free play. When spinning the wheels also check for any wobble or out-of-roundness of the wheels. If you find any problems, replace the wheelset—this problem is very difficult to correct.

When all checks are complete, set the truck on some track and push it down the track using light finger pressure on the bolster. You will feel any remaining wheel problems with your finger. Now push the truck to see how freely it rolls. HO scale and larger trucks should easily roll several feet. N and Z scale will roll considerably less because there is less mass to overcome friction. Truck rolling quality will vary slightly, even on identical trucks. This is no cause for concern, since there is virtually no difference in the force needed to pull these cars. It *is* cause for concern in HO and larger scales if the truck rolls only several inches and stops. If

Fig. 4-7. You can upgrade the snap-in truck to a screw-mounted truck. First you'll have to plug the large hole. Here a piece of styrene tube has been cemented into the hole.

you notice tightness, go back and deal with the problem as I explained previously. In N and Z scale, as long as the axles turn freely, there should be no problems because the small mass of these pieces will not allow the cars to roll very far.

How the truck is mounted to the frame is just as important as the truck itself. If you have a small layout and operate infrequently, cars with friction-pin mounting may not pose a problem. If you want reliable consistent performance from your rolling stock, however, screws are the only way to go.

Many manufacturers of high-quality rolling stock use screws for mounting trucks. A screw provides both strength and adjustment; the latter is a most important consideration for optimum performance. Some manufacturers use a friction pin to hold trucks in place. While this may be adequate in N scale, screws would be better. In larger scales, screws should be mandatory.

Converting a car from friction-pin to screw truck mounting is not difficult. In N scale the conversion is usually easy. The mounting pin on most

N scale equipment is roughly the size of a 2-56 screw, the size of screw most often used. Remove the truck and drill a no. 50 hole through the bolster center plate opening. Now run a 2-56 tap through both holes to cut screw threads. Clean any flash from the center plate and mount the trucks with ³⁄₁₆", 2-56 roundhead screws. Upgrading truck mounting to screw mounting is covered later in this chapter.

In HO or larger scales, converting to a screw mount may be a little more involved. As in N scale, a 2-56 screw is a good choice for mounting the trucks. A problem arises if the friction pin is larger in diameter than the 2-56 screws that will be used. The solution is to plug the original hole with a piece of styrene rod or tube. A piece of plastic runner found in most styrene model kits will work well. Another option is to use commercially available pieces. Evergreen makes a variety of tube and rod sizes. Use the size that fits the mounting hole (fig. 4-7); if none fits the bill, sand down the next larger size until it fits tightly into the hole. Apply liquid cement to secure the plugs. After the cement has dried, cut the plug off

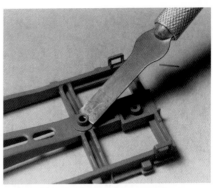

Fig. 4-10. You'll usually have to remove part of the center plate lip in order to tighten one truck adequately. A no. 17 X-acto knife works well for this, as shown.

Fig. 4-8. Cut the plug flush with the top of the bolster and drill and tap it for a 2-56 screw, which you'll use to mount the truck.

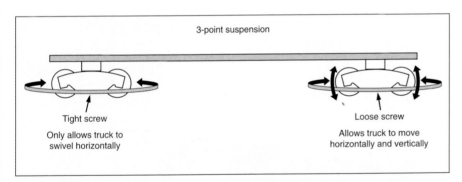

3-point suspension

Tight screw
Only allows truck to swivel horizontally

Loose screw
Allows truck to move horizontally and vertically

Fig. 4-9. This illustration shows how to set up the three-point truck system. Secure one truck so that it can turn in only one plane, and leave the other truck looser to allow the car to negotiate uneven track.

flush with the top of the center plate, drill no. 50 holes in the center of the plug, and use a 2-56 tap to cut the screw threads (fig. 4-8).

Before mounting the trucks, be sure to remove any flash or other stray material on the center plate.

To mount your trucks properly, you should use what is called three-point installation, as illustrated in fig. 4-9. In this method one truck is installed slightly loose. Here, "loose" means able not only to swivel but to rock front to back and side to side. The other screw is turned tight, then loosened just enough that the truck can pivot freely but not turn in any other

axis. Some manufacturers have a cast-on raised lip on their center plate to keep the truck properly centered. Often this lip extends slightly higher than the bottom of the truck mounting hole when the truck is installed. The extra height keeps you from tightening one screw properly. Figure 4-10 shows how you can remove part of this lip with a no. 17 X-acto blade so that you can tighten the screw properly. This type of mounting will allow the trucks to negotiate uneven track but will not allow the car to rock from side to side unprototypically.

Check the couplers. The subject of couplers is wide and varied. Which

coupler you choose is determined by what type of operating you plan to do. In HO scale most equipment comes with the standard X-2F or horn-hook coupler. Most N scale comes with the Rapido-type coupler, while Z scale comes with either Micro-Trains or Märklin. Larger scales usually come with the particular manufacturer's own style of coupler.

HO scale modelers have the easiest time dealing with couplers, since most manufacturers have settled on a standard-size coupler box. Most of the time, all modelers have to do to change couplers is remove the unwanted coupler, drop in the coupler of their choice, close the box, and start operating.

If you plan to use the X2F coupler that comes with most HO rolling stock, it is worthwhile to check the coupler height. Do this by using the coupler height slot on the NMRA gauge (fig. 4-11). Set the gauge on the rails and see how the height of the slot compares with the actual coupler height. It should be reasonably close to the center of the gauge slot. If not, it should be adjusted, or you may have unscheduled uncouplings. Make slight adjustments in height by bending the shank of the coupler between the coupler head and the pivot mounting in the direction needed. Give the shank a good bend.

The flexibility of the plastic will return most of the bend, but the shank should take a slight set and stay where you need it. Repeat this until the coupler is the proper height. To compensate for larger differences in height, follow the examples given in the next section dealing with knuckle couplers.

Check the trip pin height as well. If the trip pin hangs below the height of the rails, it will snag trackwork and cause derailments. Lay your NMRA gauge flat on the rails and push the coupler over it. The trip pin should not touch the gauge. If it does, trim the pin until it clears (fig. 4-12).

Remove any flash on the coupler, especially around the knuckle. Also check the range of motion. The coupler should deflect to the side quite easily and return when released. If the coupler swing is tight or binds, remove the coupler lid and check for flash or any other foreign material. If that doesn't help, apply a little powdered graphite as a lubricant. Never use any type of oil or grease on a coupler, only a dry lubricant. If you cannot get the coupler to operate reliably you can buy new couplers. They are even available in their own draft gear box. Installation of a new draft gear box is covered in the section on knuckle couplers.

While the X-2F coupler is functional, it is difficult to uncouple and is unprototypically large. What's more, the lateral spring pressure exerted can cause operational problems. The solution to all these problems is replacement with a knuckle-type coupler. Until recent years the only knuckle-type coupler available was the Kadee, but that has changed. Several companies now offer similar compatible couplers. In fact, some manufacturers are even offering these new couplers as standard equipment on their rolling stock. While the modeler does now have options beside the Kadee coupler, Kadee still offers the greatest variety of shank lengths and types. This man-

Fig. 4-11. Check the height of an HO scale X2F coupler by comparing it to the slot in the NMRA gauge.

Fig. 4-12. Check the X2F trip pin height by laying the NMRA gauge across the track. If the pin snags the gauge, you'll have to trim the pin to clear it. If you allow the trip pin to hang below the rail height, it will snag trackwork and possibly derail the car.

ufacturer also offers a very complete coupler conversion guide, which aids the modeler in converting to better couplers on many types of locomotives and rolling stock. Figure 4-13 shows the dramatic improvement when the X2F coupler is replaced with a knuckle coupler, in this case a Kadee no. 5.

The knuckle-type coupler is easy to install in most rolling stock. Before you start to install it, though, look closely at how the coupler pocket lid is held in place, because this varies from manufacturer to manufacturer. Some use screws to hold the lid, Walthers uses a center friction pin, and Athearn uses a metal lid that clips in place. In the interest of strength and reliability, use a screw to hold the lid in place. Converting nonscrew covers to screw covers is not difficult. For Walthers and similar friction-pin cars, remove the mounting pin and use it as a guide in locating and drilling a hole that will clear whatever screw size you use. A 2-56 screw would be a good choice for HO scale. Now drill a no. 50 hole through the coupler pocket pivot and use a 2-56 tap to cut the threads. Figure 4-14 shows a before and after modification. You can now install your coupler.

The Athearn coupler pocket is a little more difficult to modify. The center pivot is slightly smaller in diameter than the Walthers pivot. If you drill it and tap it for a 2-56 screw, it might split. One solution is to use a smaller 1-80 screw. The other is to remove the cast-on center pivot and use a slightly shortened Kadee draft gear box top cover with the center boss left in place and the "ears" cut off. Since the center boss opening will clear a 2-56 screw, you'll only have to cut threads for the 2-56 screw into the base of the Athearn coupler pocket. Figure 4-15 shows a modified Athearn pocket with the slightly modified Kadee cover next to a stock unit. If the threads are stripped out of the thin pocket base, you'll have to cement a styrene backer plate to the top of the coupler box and drill and tap it for the 2-56 screw. Install the coupler of your choice, screw the lid down, and your modification is complete.

Installing knuckle couplers is easy and takes only a matter of seconds on some units; checking for proper adjustment, however, takes more time. The first thing to check is freedom of movement. The coupler should swing easily from side to side. The only resistance should be that of the centering spring. There should be no binding or tightness in its range of motion. If there is, check the mounting screw for excess tightness or for flash or rough spots in the coupler

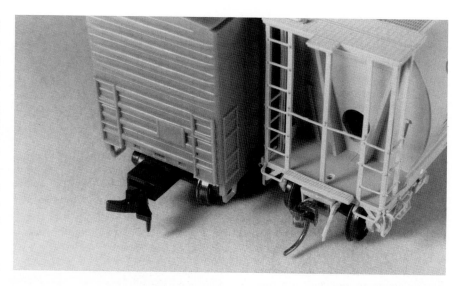

Fig. 4-13. While the X2F coupler is functional, it neither works as well nor looks as good as a knuckle coupler. The Atlas boxcar on the left is shown with an X2F coupler as received from the manufacturer, while the InterMountain covered hopper on the right has been upgraded with a Kadee no. 5 coupler.

Fig. 4-14. Secure coupler lids with a screw if at all possible. This photo shows a stock Atlas car with a pin-mounted coupler plate. The Walthers car on the right came standard with the same pin mount. It was modified by drilling a hole in the coupler plate and drilling and tapping a 2-56 hole in the coupler pivot post. The screw will make for a stronger mount, as well as allow for easy access to the coupler for maintenance.

box. Do not proceed until the coupler moves freely.

The next thing to check is the coupler height. A Kadee (HO) or Micro-Trains (N) coupler height gauge works best at this task for all manufacturers' couplers. Figure 4-16 shows a Micro-Trains gauge with a properly adjusted knuckle coupler. If there is a significant deviation in height, you can adjust the car height, adjust only the coupler box height, or use a Kadee offset shank coupler to make up the difference.

You can raise the car height by adding thin washers between the trucks and bolsters (fig. 4-17). Kadee offers an assortment of washers to accomplish this, or you can make your own from various thicknesses of styrene. Using washers can cause problems, however, as each one that you add will introduce a little slack or "give" to the center plate. When you attempt to tighten the one screw properly for three-point suspension, this "give" will not allow you to tighten the screw properly, and the car may rock. A more permanent and solid solution is to add the needed thickness of styrene sheet. Secure it to the bolster with liquid cement (on plastic) or cyanoacrylate (on metal). Another way is to use part of a Kadee coupler mounting box as raw material. Figure 4-16 shows a dissected coupler box being installed on an Athearn 54-foot covered hopper. On this particular car, the new center plate will bring the coupler up to perfect height; it replaces the "shoulder" that was removed.

Lowering the car or coupler height is a little more difficult. There are two ways to do it. Lowering the bolster center plate by removing excess material with a file is the quickest, but you must be sure to keep the bolster surface in plane with the rest of the frame. If you don't, the truck will not sit square and the car will lean, or the truck will tip toward the front or back, causing wheel contact problems. The other way is to remove or replace the coupler box and lower the mounting area. If you are careful you can saw off the cast-on box, add the needed material, and cement the box back in place. If you ruin the box or simply want to replace it, you can use the Kadee mounting box, which fits Kadee couplers perfectly. Add the coupler box after building up the mounting area by the necessary amount (fig. 4-19).

After you adjust coupler height, the trip pin is next. Again, the Kadee coupler height gauge is perfect for this. The trip pin should be slightly above rail height. Obviously, if it is

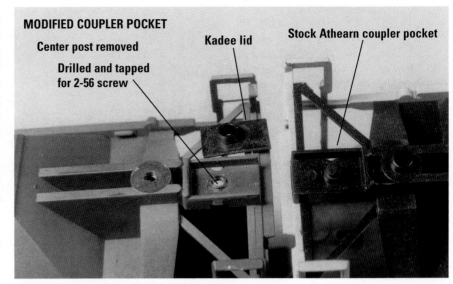

MODIFIED COUPLER POCKET

Center post removed

Drilled and tapped for 2-56 screw

Kadee lid

Stock Athearn coupler pocket

Fig. 4-15. It is a little more difficult to modify an Athearn coupler pocket. The car on the left has the stock Athearn coupler pocket, while the car on the right has a the modified coupler pocket, as explained in the text.

Fig. 4-16. A properly adjusted Micro-Trains coupler in N scale. While the components in N scale are only about half the size of their HO counterparts, you must adjust them to the same close tolerances to ensure reliable operation.

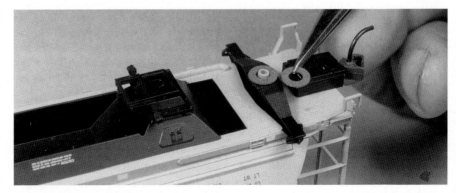

Fig. 4-17. Raise the coupler height by adding small washers to the truck bolster, which raises the height of the car.

Fig. 4-18. The trimmed Kadee top cover is being added to the center plate on this Athearn PS 54-foot covered hopper.

Styrene shim used to lower coupler pocket

Fig. 4-19. If the coupler is too high, lower it by cementing styrene shims to the body before adding the coupler box.

too low and snags trackwork, it will cause derailments. If it is too high, it will not uncouple reliably automatically. To adjust the trip pin you must bend it in the needed direction. Do this with either needle-nose pliers or Kadee trip-pin pliers. Figures 4-20 and 4-21 show the proper way to adjust the pin using a pair of Kadee pliers.

When everything is adjusted, test the coupler for proper operation using an uncoupling magnet installed on a piece of track. When you move the coupler over the magnet, the coupler should deflect to the side and the knuckle should open. If it doesn't, there is probably a bind somewhere. Find it and correct it. You can also use a small amount of powdered graphite as a lubricant. Use scrapings from pencil lead, or buy the material in a handy applicator bottle offered by Kadee. You only need a little. Never use any type of liquid lubricant on the coupler. It will only collect dirt and ruin operation.

Occasionally, while you're handling a coupler, you may lose the tiny knuckle spring. Every pack of Kadee couplers comes with spares, so you can replace any lost ones. Because of their small size, it may be difficult to install a new spring. The method I use most often to replace a lost spring is to take the tip of a no. 11 X-acto blade and push it into the tighter coils at the

end of the spring (fig. 4-22). Place the other end over one of the "fingers" that hold the spring, push downward to compress the spring, and slip the other end over the other finger. It may take a little practice and a few lost springs to master this technique.

N scale modelers have two basic types of couplers, the Rapido and the Micro-Trains. Figure 4-23 shows a comparison of the two types. The Rapido is the standard coupler of most N scale equipment. Only Micro-Trains equipment comes with the Micro-Trains Magne-Matic coupler installed. The Rapido is not very attractive, being grossly over scale

size, but it does work well. It couples and stays together very well. Uncoupling can be a little tedious, however, because one coupler knuckle must be lifted over the other. The first thing to check on the Rapido is the ease and smoothness of motion. Since the coupler pivots upward to couple, lift the coupler with a small screwdriver. It should lift easily (fig. 4-24). If it seems tight or, worse, if you lift up the end of the car, the coupler needs attention. Check for flash in the slot where the coupler shank moves (fig. 4-25). If nothing is apparent, remove the coupler from the draft gear box. Push the coupler

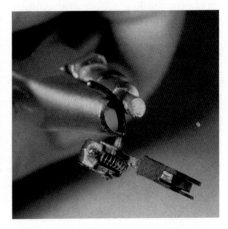

Fig. 4-20. Kadee trip pin pliers work well to adjust the trip pin height. Position the trip pin and squeeze as shown to raise the pin height.

Fig. 4-21. To lower the trip pin height, position the pin as shown and squeeze.

Fig. 4-22. The small knuckle spring can be lost in HO scale Kadee couplers. Replacing it can be a tedious job. Try to pick one up with the tip of a knife. Slip one end over one of the spring-retaining "fingers" on the coupler. Push lightly to compress the spring until the other end clears the remaining finger, and remove the tip of the knife.

Fig. 4-23. The N scale Rapido coupler is grossly oversize compared to the Micro-Trains coupler on the right, but it does work well.

Fig. 4-24. To check for ease of operation, lift the Rapido coupler. It should rise easily and definitely not lift the wheels off the track. Look into any tightness or binding that you notice.

in and turn 90 degrees. You should now be able to remove the coupler, but be careful not to lose the spring. Inspect both the coupler and the draft gear box for flash. Reassemble the coupler and check again. If motion still is tight, remove the coupler again, file some material from the slot on the draft gear box, and try again. It may take some tinkering to loosen a stubborn coupler, so be patient. Sometimes a little powdered graphite applied where the coupler pivots will improve operation. As I've said before and will say again, no oil or grease, only dry lubricant.

Adding Micro-Trains or similar style couplers is a great operational and visual improvement. Unfortunately, N scale cars do not have a standard-size coupler box. Converting to Micro-Trains couplers requires complete removal of the Rapido coupler and draft gear box. Most N scale equipment has the coupler mounted directly on the truck (talgo style). Since Micro-Trains offers talgo trucks with Micro-Trains couplers already installed (fig. 4-26), replacement can be as easy as replacing the trucks. You may also decide to body-mount the

Micro-Trains couplers, as is done on most HO equipment (fig. 4-27). For a good solid mounting, mount the couplers with a screw. Mount the coupler right to the bottom of the underframe and use the same techniques to adjust height that I previously described for HO. Again, proper adjustment is very important for reliable operation. Use a Micro-Trains coupler height gauge

and follow the example in the HO scale section.

Larger scales often feature couplers that are unique to each manufacturer. Again, Kadee makes couplers to fit most scales; the type of coupler a modeler uses will be dictated by each modeler's needs. Mount Kadee couplers to larger scale units by using the methods

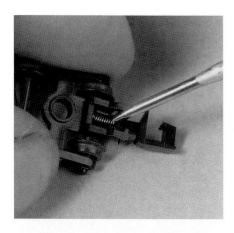

Fig. 4-25. Check for flash in and around the coupler shank and the edges of the coupler box. If the coupler operation does not improve, remove the coupler by pushing the coupler in to compress the spring, and twist the coupler 90 degrees. The coupler will rise out of the top of the coupler box. Be careful not to lose the spring. Check all surfaces for flash or a tight fit and trim until the coupler operates easily.

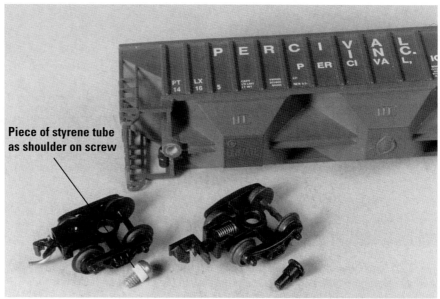

Piece of styrene tube as shoulder on screw

Fig. 4-26. It's easy to replace Rapido-equipped talgo trucks with Micro-Trains-equipped talgo trucks. On this Red Caboose covered hopper, use a screw to attach the truck instead of the friction pin. The 2-56 screw does not have the wider shoulder that the friction pin has, so you'll have to cut one from ⅛" Evergreen tube as shown in the photo.

already described for HO and N scale equipment.

Weight the car. The weight of rolling stock is very important for reliable operation. The NMRA has come up with a set of weight standards for a number of scales. The standard establishes a base weight for each car and adds more weight on the basis of length per inch of car. Many cars off the shelf are too light. While most cars end up on the layout without additional weight, a little extra effort to bring a car up to standards will reward the modeler with more reliable operation. The NMRA has an RP or recommended practice concerning car weights. In HO scale the base weight is one ounce. For each inch of car, add ½ ounce more of weight. Using a typical 50-foot boxcar as an example, with a length of 7 inches the weight should be 7 x .5 oz = 3.5 ounces plus the 1 ounce of base weight, which would equal 4.5 ounces.

The basic rule of thumb when adding weight is to keep it as low as possible and keep the weight centered in the car. Keeping the weight low keeps the center of gravity low and makes the car more stable. Keeping the weight centered keeps equal weight on both trucks.

There are many methods of adding weight. Figure 4-28 shows some commercially available options. Some manufacturers offer stick-on weights in a variety of weights that are easy to add to a car (fig. 4-29). Simply add the proper amount to bring the car up to the correct weight. You can use lead shot or moldable lead weights to add weight in tight quarters. Figure 4-30 shows lead shot added to a covered hopper. Add the proper amount of weight and secure the shot by flooding the area with thickened cyanoacrylate.

The commercially available products are easy to use but rather pricey. One can use any heavy material to do the same thing. Washers, nuts, and thin steel strap cut to length are all possibilities. Attach the extra weight with epoxy or silicone sealer for maximum holding power. You can use thickened cyanoacrylate, but a sharp jolt could cause the weight to break loose. You don't want a loose weight sliding around inside the car.

Another way to add weight is to use a metal alloy with a low melting temperature. Several manufacturers offer such material. You can pour this material directly into brass or other metal rolling stock. To use on plastic models, you'll have to make some sort of simple mold in which to pour the material, since the 150°–180° melting temperature will soften or melt most plastic. Make the mold of aluminum foil. Take a piece of foil and push it into the area where the weight is needed. When removed it should retain the shape of the area. Fill the foil mold with the molten material. After it cools, remove the foil and install the new weight with silicone sealer or epoxy.

Adding additional weight is easy on a boxcar or covered hopper because the weight is concealed under a large body. Other cars may not be so easy. Any open car will be more difficult, since most areas of the car are visible. It can be a real challenge to add enough weight to

Fig. 4-27. Body-mounting Micro-Trains couplers in N scale is quite easy. Since most cars are equipped with talgo-mounted couplers, cut the coupler off the truck, then drill and tap a hole in the bottom of the car to attach the coupler.

Fig. 4-28. Several types of commercial weights. In the top package are lead BBs, in the middle are tape-mounted "break-off" weights, and at the bottom is moldable lead putty that can shaped to fit odd or irregular places.

these cars. One way is to model the car with a load. Whether you model coal in hopper cars or scrap in a gondola, you can hide the weight below the load. Adding weight to a tank car can be a little tricky. If you're building the car from a kit, you'll have to add any additional weight before assembling the tank. Adding more weight to such a closed car may be impossible after assembly.

You'll have to use creativity to add weight to some cars. Empty stack cars or container cars are a perfect example of this. These cars are virtual skeletons without containers, so adding any weight inconspicuously is a challenge. About the only place to add weight is in the truck area. Obviously, adding containers to these cars would be an easy answer—just be sure to add weight only to the lower car to keep the center of gravity low.

There are a group of modelers who practice what is known as "live load" modeling. These modelers load their cars prototypically with whatever commodity the cars actually haul (coal, iron ore, and so on). This makes for wonderfully realistic and challenging operation but can be a mechanical problem. Not only can the increased weight cause some

very realistic and messy derailments, but the needle-point axles can drastically wear into the truck sideframes. If you are considering such a "live load" operation, you should be aware of this potential problem; and if you do practice such operation, check your sideframes for excessive wear. Should the axles wear significantly into the sideframes, you'll have to replace the sideframes. One solution to this problem in HO scale would be to use Kato's new roller-bearing-style trucks. Instead of turning on needle-point "bearings," the full diameter of the axle turns on friction pads, which greatly reduces the wear problem.

MAINTAINING ROLLING STOCK

Maintenance of rolling stock is not nearly as intensive as that of locomotives, but you must give thought to the care of your car fleet. Many modelers do not worry about car maintenance and only deal with the issue when there are problems. Most often, time spent doing preventive maintenance will be less than that spent dealing with problems that result from lack of maintenance. And there will be fewer operational headaches. Items that you should check include wheel dirt, wheel gauge, truck motion, coupler and trip

pin height, and coupler operation. While you should check and adjust all these things before adding a piece of rolling stock to a layout, use and abuse may knock some of them out of acceptable limits.

A simple preventive maintenance program need not be time-consuming. If you have a good system, you can check all operating parts and clean the car wheels in a minute or two per car. Unless you have a huge fleet, you should easily get through your entire fleet in an evening. How often you intend to check your fleet depends on how often you operate. That must be determined by each modeler.

Keep the wheels clean. Clean rolling stock wheels are not as important as those on locomotives, where electricity must have an uninterrupted path. But they should not be ignored. Dirt left to build up on wheels will become an operational problem. Even if you clean your track and locomotive wheels religiously, if you seldom clean your rolling stock wheels, they

Fig. 4-29. Add stick-on weights in the amount you need. The weights have a peel-off paper backing that covers the adhesive. Remove the backing and apply the weight.

Fig. 4-30. Add the appropriate amount of Lead BBs to the bottom of this covered hopper. Flood thickened cyanoacrylate into the area to secure the weight. It is important to keep the weight as low as possible.

will quickly soil your track. It's kind of like scrubbing your floor and walking across the floor with muddy shoes when you're finished.

You can clean rolling stock wheels in the same way as you cleaned your locomotive wheels, except that you provide the power. Wet a small end of paper towel with WD-40 and lay it across a piece of track. It is best to have a board with several feet of track attached that is separate from your layout to do this. Roll the car through the WD-40 several times, using light finger pressure, until the dirt softens. This is indicated by the streaks of dirt on the towel. Now roll the car over a dry section of the towel to remove the dirt and WD-40. Repeat this process until the towel stays clean where the wheels roll. Figure 4-31 shows this procedure. If you do this on a regular basis it will not take much time to do each piece, since the dirt buildup will be less. The longer you wait, the longer it will take.

You can also remove the wheels from the trucks and physically wipe or scrape the material off, but this requires a lot of handling, which may result in damage.

Adjust the wheels, trucks, and couplers. Check the trucks to make sure that they pivot easily and are properly adjusted for the three-point system. Make any necessary adjustments. Use your NMRA gauge to check the wheel gauge and correct any out-of-gauge wheels.

If you use Kadee or similar couplers, set the car on a piece of track and check for proper coupler and trip pin height. Some couplers have a tendency to sag slightly after extended use. While the coupler knuckle height may be within limits, the trip pin may now snag the top of the gauge. Bend the pin up to clear the gauge. Check the coupler for smooth operation, full range of motion, and automatic centering. If you use the delayed uncoupling feature, spot the car over an

uncoupling magnet and check for proper coupler deflection. Some couplers, it seems, want to be difficult and don't deflect properly over track magnets. The problem could be a slight bind, a bucking centering spring, or dirt. Open the coupler box and check for foreign material or rough spots on the coupler lid, coupler shank, or center pivot that will not allow proper motion. Next, check the coupler spring itself; it may be weak or bent. If nothing seems out of line, try a new spring. On some of the newer knuckle couplers, the springs are two small prongs or "whiskers" that provide the centering action. Check them for problems. Since they are cast as part of the coupler, it would be best to replace the coupler if there are problems. Patience will solve any coupler problem.

FINE-TUNING ROLLING STOCK

Replace the wheels. While most manufacturers' trucks and wheels are perfectly usable and will provide many years of trouble-free operation, some modelers choose to upgrade these parts. A number of companies offer high-quality replacement wheels and complete trucks for a variety of rolling stock. The primary improvement from such an upgrade comes in the form of metal wheels, which are more durable and have a more accurate profile. Another benefit may be more visual accuracy. Most mass-produced rolling stock comes with the standard 33-inch scale wheels. While this size is accurate for prototype 70-ton rolling stock, most modern freight cars are 100-ton capacity and ride on 36-inch wheels. Some intermodal equipment even comes with 28-inch wheels. While most modelers will live with the 33-inch wheels, those who want closer-to-prototype appearance will want to add wheels of the correct size.

The easiest and cheapest way to get metal wheel performance is to simply replace the wheels in your trucks. Several companies offer wheelsets in 28-, 33-, and 36-inch diameter that will fit most truck frames. Before installing the wheels, check the gauge with your NMRA gauge and adjust if needed. Most metal wheelsets come with a black finish. To represent the polished-metal look of the prototype wheel tread more realistically, use a small circular wire brush in a motor tool and remove it (fig. 4-32).

If you currently have a layout on which you run a car fleet with plastic wheels and you want to upgrade to metal wheels, there is something you should be aware of. Metal wheels are noisy. While the click of metal wheels over metal track joints may have a very "railroady" appeal to the modeler, if you run long trains your consist will generate a lot more noise. While this may not make any difference to you, be aware of the fact.

Replace the trucks. The next step beyond changing wheels is to replace the entire truck. The modeler has several options when replacing trucks. If accuracy is important, select the proper truck style and wheel diameter for the type of car you are modeling, if possible. Another consideration is the type of mechanical operation you desire. There are two choices here, the rigid-frame truck, which is the type that most rolling stock comes with, and the sprung-equalized truck. Both work well.

For simplicity and usually lower cost the rigid-frame trucks work just fine. There is little to no maintenance, and most truck sideframes are very well detailed. Several trucks offered by Kato are the exception to the lower price. These are exquisitely detailed rigid-frame trucks that ride on metal wheels. The star of the line is their Barber S-2 roller bearing truck. What sets this truck apart is the rotating axle end caps. If you watch prototype trains, you will have noticed this detail on roller-bearing-equipped trucks. While Kato is not the first to offer this detail, it is the first to build a truck that rolls as well

Fig. 4-31. Clean car wheels in the same way as locomotive wheels. Apply WD-40 to the end of a piece of paper towel. Roll the car through it until the dirt dissolves. Then roll the car over a dry section of towel to remove the WD-40.

Fig. 4-32. A wire brush in a motor tool works well for removing paint and polishing metal wheel treads.

as any needle-point axle truck. While the trucks are somewhat pricey, this feature will add that final touch to a well-detailed car.

The sprung-equalized truck can add another dimension to a piece of rolling stock. While the springing is not really necessary because the weight of a car is not much of a factor, it is the equalization that will give a car a little extra prototype animation. An added benefit is that the trucks will negotiate rough spots in trackwork because all the wheels will remain in contact with the rail. The model sprung-equalized trucks are assembled just like their real-life counterparts. The ends of the bolster fit into an opening in the sideframes and the whole thing is held together by the pressure of the truck springs. Neat!

If your old trucks were mounted with screws, you can use the same screws to mount the new ones. Screw-type mountings vary from manufacturer to manufacturer. Most use some type of 2-56 screw, which is fine. In HO scale Model Die Casting or MDC uses a self-tapping screw to

secure the trucks to the frame. It works well in most cases. Sometimes, if the screw has been overtightened and has to be backed out for proper adjustment, the screw can work loose and fall out. This has happened several times to me and has caused some very prototypical derailments when the truck and car decided to go in different directions. In the interest of reliability and standardization I replace the MDC screws—and in fact all non–2-56 screws, regardless of manufacturer—with 2-56 screws, drilling and tapping the underframes as needed. In larger scales you may need to use larger screws such as 4-40s, because the 2-56 head may slip through the mounting hole or because you may need additional strength. Modifying nonstandard or friction pin mountings was covered earlier in this chapter.

After you add new trucks, there are several things you should check carefully. It is most important that the tight truck (see fig. 4-9) be perfectly lined up with the underbody or in the same plane as the frame of the car. The most troublesome misalignment is when the truck tips forward or backward. The low set of wheels will be in good contact, while the high set may hardly touch the rails, if at all. This end will easily ride up over any rough spot or track joint and derail the car. If the truck is tipped to one side, the wheels may be in good contact, but the car will lean to one side rather unprototypically. Figure 4-33 illustrates these problems and shows how to remedy them.

There are two causes for misalignment. First, the screw may not be square with the body bolster. Second, the bolster itself may not be square or may have some flash that prevents the truck from seating properly. The easiest solution is to tighten the other truck to see if it lines up better and leave the misaligned truck as the loose one. If the problem still persists, you'll have to file the bolster to square it. Do this with care to get everything square. Remove only a small amount of material at a time, screw the truck into place, and check it. Repeat this until the car sits straight.

Relocate the couplers. In rolling stock there are two types of coupler installation, the body mount and the "talgo" mount. The body mount is self-explanatory: The coupler box containing the coupler is attached in some manner to the body. This is how prototype couplers are attached, and for modeling purposes it is usually the best method. In the talgo mount, the couplers are attached to the truck. This type of mounting is most common on "train set" equipment in HO scale. Most N scale rolling stock has the talgo mounting, and in larger scale tinplate equipment it is almost universal.

Mounting couplers on the truck is a concession to the sharp curves usually found on small layouts. Because the coupler pivots with the truck, the coupler will be close to the center of the track regardless of the sharpness of the curves, making coupling easier. That is the good news. The bad news is that this type of coupler arrangement can make cars more likely to derail, especially in HO

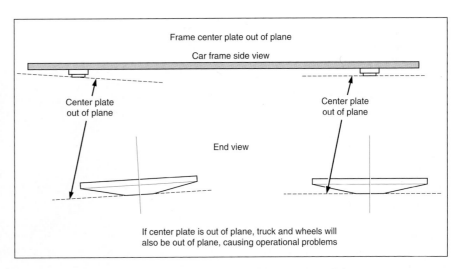

Fig. 4-33. When replacing trucks or working on the bolster center plate, make sure that the center plate is square with the frame, or the truck will not ride in plane with the rails.

and other scales in which the wheel flange is reasonably close to scale. The pulling or pushing forces on the coupler are transmitted through the trucks and then to the frame of the car. In short trains these forces are not all that great and are not much of a problem; but try running a dozen or more cars, throw in some steep grades, and you'll encounter problems. This system does work reasonably well in N scale and tinplate where the wheel flanges are proportionally much larger.

While this system has its difficulties, you can adjust cars to lessen the likelihood of problems. One very important consideration is car weight. If you follow NMRA standards for weight, the cars will track better and be less likely to climb the rails. If you mount the trucks carefully using the three-point system and make sure the wheels are in proper gauge and adjustment, you can improve the reliability of this system. Kadee even offers HO scale trucks with its own coupler talgo-mounted for those who want such a system.

There is nothing wrong with mixing talgo- and body-mounted couplers on a layout. There may possibly be some mismatching when you try to couple the two types of cars

on sharp curves, but that is about it.

Even serious HO modelers may have to resign themselves to some talgo or swiveling type of coupler on longer passenger and freight cars unless they have the luxury of very wide-radius curves. Athearn's 86-foot boxcars and 89- and 85-foot flatcars have a coupler swiveling system in which the turning truck turns the coupler. In theory this should work fine, but in reality the truck movement is hampered by the coupler's swiveling "fingers." These cars are difficult to run on anything but wide curves anyway. The added burden to the trucks of having to swing the coupler extension makes these cars an operational headache.

To improve the operation of these cars you have two options. If you have wide curves (at least 30" radius in HO scale, and 36" would be better), stationary coupler pockets would cause few problems. Mount the coupler box to the floor of the car by using a screw. A-Line offers another option. A cast-metal part provides both additional weight and a stationary coupler pocket. Installing this part also results in a more prototypically accurate car end.

For smaller-radius curves you must have some allowance for coupler swing, or the coupler overhang on curves will literally pull shorter cars right off the rails. Figure 4-34 shows a simple yet effective swinging coupler. Remove the "fingers" from the coupler mounting and use a piece of brass wire bent as shown as a coupler guide. The coupler should swivel freely inside the guide but should not be able to sag. The only drawback to this method is that the coupler will not self-center. With a little extra work you can add a self-center feature by using two pieces of .015" or ¹⁄₆₄" piano wire mounted as shown in fig. 4-35. Bend the wire into a slight curve so that each side exerts a small amount of pressure on the sides of the draft gear box. It may take some adjusting to get equal pressure on both sides. This method is similar to the coupler centering arrangement on Walthers autorack, which works very well. Speaking of Walthers, that company offers its swinging coupler as a kit that can be installed on the Athearn 85-foot flats, 86-foot hi-cubes, and any other long car that would benefit from them. Figure 4-36 shows the kit installed on an 85-foot flat. The only difficult part of the installation is that the car weight must be notched to clear the mounting screws.

REPAIRING ROLLING STOCK

You should now have a fleet of well-adjusted, smoothly rolling, clean cars that operate nearly flawlessly on your layout. While I have repeatedly stressed the importance of mechanical operation, you also need a good-looking piece of rolling stock, or the illusion is ruined. Each complements the other. During the course of operating a model empire, whether it's a small oval or a sprawling layout, you will most likely encounter some damage to your fleet of rolling stock. While some damage may occur as the result of derailments, the most likely source of damage is from careless handling. Broken or damaged detail parts are the most common prob-

Wire bracket to support coupler

Fig. 4-34. A wire bracket keeps extended draft gear on an Athearn 86-foot boxcar from sagging.

lems. The smaller and more numerous the details, the more likely they are to become damaged by careless handling. Should parts become broken off, it is usually possible to cement them back into place without too much problem. If the part is very small, or if a small mounting pin has been broken off, it is possible to strengthen the joint when replacing the part. Drill a small hole in the broken-off part and in the corresponding location on the car. Use a similar-sized piece of brass wire and thickened cyanoacrylate to reattach the part to the car. When it's dry, the joint should be stronger than the original. Figure 4-37 shows a brake wheel replaced by this method.

Deal with damaged parts on an individual basis. The damaged part could be broken or cracked ladder rungs, a roof walk, stirrup steps, or any other added or cast-on part. The easiest repair uses liquid cement. Hold or push the damaged part back into place and apply cement to the joints of the cracked or broken part.

If the part is too severely damaged to be repaired, you'll have to

Piano wire used as centering spring

Fig. 4-35. A piece of piano wire cemented to the draft gear extension as explained in the text will serve as a centering spring on the swiveling draft gear.

remove it and replace it. Finding a replacement part may be as easy as ordering a new part or as complicated as building a new one from scratch. Another source may be cannibalizing a part from a retired unit in your scrap box. After finding a replacement part, determine how it will be mounted before removing the old part. You may have to leave on part of the mounting, especially if the new part comes from another source. After determining to mount the new part, remove the broken part, doing as little additional damage to the surrounding area as possible. Test-fit the new part, making any necessary changes, then paint the part to match the original.

Stirrup steps located at the lower corners of most cars are very vulnerable to damage. These are most often cast-on parts and do not take much abuse. Often one step is damaged or destroyed, but replacing just one step doesn't look that good. A-Line makes several styles of replacement HO scale metal steps. If one step needs replacement, in the interest of looks it is best to replace all four. Simply slice off the cast-on steps flush with the bottom of the car and drill mounting holes to position the new steps (fig. 4-38). In some cases the lower edge of the body is too thin to drill, so cement scrap styrene to the inside of the shell as a backer and then drill to mount the steps. Secure the new steps with cyanoacrylate and paint them to match the car. If A-Line steps are not the type of step you need or if you model some other scale, you could bend new matching steps from Detail Associates flat brass wire. Mount them in the same way. In N scale you could simply use small-diameter wire, since the flatness of the step will not be noticeable. In this case repairing a broken part will actually result in an improved model; the new metal steps will be more scale in appearance than the cast-on parts.

Painting a replacement part the correct color may be a challenge, since each manufacturer's color may be a little different. Test-paint a piece of scrap before painting the actual part. You may have to do a little mixing to achieve a correct or close match. A slight difference may not be noticeable, especially if a model is weathered. Allow the painted part to dry.

WORKBENCH TIP: Cleaning Your Rolling Stock

Cleaning your rolling stock is more for appearance than operation. Your cars will accumulate a variety of unwanted deposits, and unfortunately the deposits do not resemble prototypical weathering. Dust is probably the biggest culprit. Remove it with a small, soft brush. Gently brush the dust off the car, taking care to get it in small or narrow crevices. Be careful not to break off small or delicate details.

Dirt or fingerprints are another matter, since these deposits are not so easy to remove. The best way to deal with them is by prevention. Always handle your cars with clean hands. After eating greasy food or snacks, always wash your hands before you handle anything on your layout. Oil or grease on your fingers can leave an unsightly smudge or fingerprint. Handle your cars along the edges, or if possible in an area that's hard to see.

If the worst happens and your car gets dirty or has an unsightly fingerprint, first call the FBI and have the culprit charged with vandalism. You thought graffiti was bad. Can you imagine a greasy fingerprint on the side of a car blown up to life size? Seriously, if you can remove the body from the underframe, try washing it in warm water with a little liquid dishwashing detergent added. If you cannot remove the body and such immersion is not possible, try dabbing the area with a cotton swab dampened with dishwashing detergent and water. If your car is weathered and has been properly sealed with a clear finish, the sealer will protect the finish adequately, so there shouldn't be a problem. Use a light touch anyway.

When you have finished washing, whether by full immersion in water or spot-cleaning, always blot the water drops from the surface. If they are left to dry on their own they will probably leave unsightly spots that may look worse than the dirt you just washed from the car.

Fig. 4-36. Walthers offers this swiveling coupler from its 89-foot autorack as a separate item. Here one is installed on an Athearn 86-foot flatcar.

Fig. 4-37. Reinforce small broken-off parts with a brass pin. Drill a hole into a broken-off brake wheel and insert a small pin of a corresponding size into it. Drill a similar-size hole into its intended location on the car. Use thickened cyanoacrylate to reattach the part to the car.

Fig. 4-38. Stirrup steps are easily broken off. Here on the left a brass step made by A-Line replaces the stirrup step on the 50-foot single-door MDC car. The result is an even better looking step than the original step on the car on the right.

If your car was weathered originally, you may want to weather the part as well to match the surrounding area of the car before you attach it. Another option is to leave the part unweathered or a slightly different color to represent a repaired part on the prototype. It is not uncommon to see repaired or replaced parts on a real railroad car, and the difference in color and weathering makes them quite noticeable.

When you're satisfied with the color, secure the new part to the car with whatever adhesive fits the situation. When the adhesive has dried, touch up any area affected by the removal of the part. A light weathering, if necessary, will blend everything together, and the repair will be complete.

Paint scratches and dings are also the result of careless handling. Touch up dings with a small brush and some matching paint, and they will hardly be noticeable. Scratches can be a little more difficult. The attempt to cover a significant scratch may be as noticeable as, if not more noticeable than, the scratch itself. To do a good job

you'll have to sand out the scratch and use an airbrush and an exact color match. Another way is to follow the prototype. When the damage is repaired on some cars, they only receive a "patch" paint job—only the affected area is repainted. Even if the original color is used for this abbreviated paint job, it is likely that the original paint has weathered and faded so it will be a slightly different color. This effect is easy to model by masking around the area and either airbrushing or carefully brush-painting the area. The result is another prototypically correct look.

Probably the most serious damage to a piece of rolling stock occurs when it is dropped to the floor or when it takes the "big plunge" in a derailment too close to the edge of the layout. While no floor is soft, except maybe some types of carpeting, a car that lands on cement is likely to have severe damage. If the car hits trucks or coupler first, the body may be spared the worst damage. (Repair of couplers and trucks was covered earlier.) If, however, a corner of the body breaks the fall,

there will be significant damage. If you choose to repair the car and not chuck it in the scrap box (remember, modelers throw nothing away—today's scrap is tomorrow's treasure), approach the repair in auto body fashion. Besides replacing any damaged parts, fill and sand to shape any dented corners and edges, just as you would fix similar damage to your car.

The first order of business is to square up the damaged corner again. A mashed corner "mushrooms" and you'll have to remove the displaced material. A file and sandpaper work well for this. After everything is square again use your favorite putty to replace the missing material. It may take several applications to build up enough material. Now use files and sandpaper to shape the putty to the proper contour, and paint to match the original color. If done well there should be no signs of your car's unscheduled encounter.

With a good program of maintenance and repair, your fleet of rolling stock will continue to operate and look as good as they did when they first turned a wheel on your layout.

Maintaining & Repairing
Your Layout

CHAPTER FIVE

You can build and maintain your locomotives and rolling stock to the highest standards, but unless you maintain your layout to similar standards, the effort is mostly wasted. Attempting to operate a poor or undermaintained layout will be frustrating and sometimes even embarrassing.

To be effective, any maintenance program must begin with good construction. Poor construction and poorly installed components will not operate reliably, regardless of the maintenance they receive. Although details of construction and track installation are beyond the scope of this book, a number of other Kalmbach books and magazine articles cover these subjects in detail.

Most modelers take great pride in their layout's appearance and take reasonable measures to prevent damage to it. But there comes a time when even the strictest preventive measures fail and some type of mishap occurs.

Sometimes layout components just plain wear out. Depending on the component and the circumstances, it may be in your best interest to repair an item rather than replace it with a new one. There are several things to consider when deciding whether to repair or replace. The cost of a new item compared to the cost of repair is one. Time is another. The cost of repairing a particular item may be significantly less than the cost of a new one, but if your modeling time is

limited, replacement makes the most sense. For some items, cost versus time is not an issue. A good example would be what to do about a worn turnout point. The cost of replacing the turnout may not be that high. But if the track is ballasted and scenery is in place, it may be better to repair the worn-out part rather than disturb the ballast and scenery. You must decide what is best in each situation.

KEEPING YOUR LAYOUT CLEAN

Your first concern should be keeping the layout environment as clean as possible. The less dirt and dust that settles on the layout, the better it is for both operational and aesthetic purposes. The effort needed to keep a layout clean depends on its location and how often it is used. Obviously, if the modeler has a choice, the ideal location for a layout—from a maintenance standpoint—is in a climate-controlled room used strictly for model railroading. The fewer the outside sources of contamination, the cleaner the layout will stay. The bottom line is that the amount of time spent on cleaning your layout will be a function of its location and the activity that takes place around it.

You can take preventive measures to decrease the amount of dirt that falls on your miniature world. If you have a small layout, a 4 x 8 or some variation, a cheap plastic dropcloth could provide considerable protection between work or operating sessions. These cloths are normally 9 x 12 feet and are made of very thin plastic, only a few mils thick. They are designed to cover floors and furniture when you're painting or doing some other messy domestic project. The best thing about them is that they cost only a buck or two. You could easily spread such a sheet over a small layout with the help of a friend, or *carefully* by yourself. The extreme thinness and lightness of this material will not damage even the most fragile items on a layout. Figure 5-1 shows a dropcloth covering a small layout. You could cover even larger areas by using more sheets. While such coverings are probably not practical on large layouts for regular use, you could use

them to cover finished areas of layouts when you're doing some messy construction on unfinished areas.

The preparation and finish of the layout area will play a big role in how quickly a layout becomes dirty and how dirty it gets. In a basement, which is a popular location for layouts, there are two big contributors, the ceiling and the floor. It is amazing how much dirt can filter through an upstairs floor. A permanent solution would be some sort of ceiling installation above the layout. Drywall, a suspended ceiling, or even paneling or plywood would fill the bill. Lacking resources for a permanent fix, a sheet of plastic stapled to the bottom of the floor joists over the layout would accomplish the same thing.

A bare concrete basement floor provides its share of dust as foot traffic slowly wears away small amounts of cement. The resulting dust is very fine and can contribute to contamination. Adding carpet or linoleum would eliminate the problem and be decorative too. A less costly solution would be to paint the floor with a paint designed for that purpose.

Clean the track. Dirty track is problem track, and the best electric-powered locomotives in the world will not run worth a darn on dirty rails. While clean track has always been a priority, it is even more important if you use DCC for train control. The rail-to-wheel pickup is not very efficient to start with. Since the DCC system must send bursts of computer-

coded information to the locomotive, it is critical that these contact points be as clean as possible.

Two main things cause track contact problems: dirt and oxidation (fig. 5-2). Dirt has many sources—airborne dust, smoke, and wheel dirt from locomotives and cars, to name a few. Oxidation is a natural process in most metals in which the metal reacts in the presence of oxygen to form a protective coating. This oxidized material acts as an insulator, which causes difficulties with electrical contact. On steel, the oxidized material is called rust.

Most model railroad rail is made from a nickel-silver alloy that oxidizes very slowly. If at all possible, you should avoid brass or steel rail. It is usually cheaper than its nickel-silver counterpart, but it oxidizes very fast and will need more cleaning. The extra cost of nickel-silver will be repaid in less maintenance.

"How do I know when to clean my track?" While it may seem like a silly question, it can have a variety of answers. One answer is when you clean your locomotive wheels. It makes no sense to clean your locomotive wheels and then run them on dirty track—no more sense than cleaning your track and running locomotives with dirty wheels. Any dirt on either will easily and quickly transfer from one to the other.

Another sign that your track needs cleaning is excessive sparking between the locomotive wheels and the track. While some sparking is normal, excessive sparking is a sign that dirt is beginning to accumulate, even though your locomotives may still run well. While some may view these sparks as a miniature fireworks show and a form of entertainment, the sparks are electrical arcs and actually burn tiny pits into the rail and wheel. These pits will provide tiny pockets in which dirt can accumulate.

Sure signs of dirt are flickering headlights, hesitation, jerking, and finally stalling. There is no point in

Fig. 5-1. A cheap painting dropcloth is great for covering small layouts.

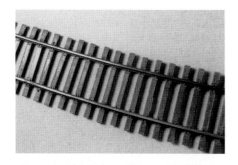

Fig. 5-2. While they are not easy to see in this photo, dirt and oxidation can ruin the performance of even the best locomotives.

trying to operate when dirt has accumulated to this point. It is time to clean the track.

There are a number of different ways to clean track. If your track is very dirty and your locomotives have difficulty running any distance, you can manually rub the accumulated material off with an eraser-type cleaning block (fig. 5-3). It is also a good idea to run the cleaning block along the inside of the rails once in a while (fig. 5-4). Dirt can accumulate here, but not as quickly as on the top of the rails. A popular type sold by Walthers is called a Bright Boy, although there are several other blocks made by different manufacturers. Even a good hard ink eraser will work just fine. My favorite is called Perfect Abrasive Track Cleaner. It is about the hardness of an ink eraser

and has a very fine abrasive. This block may be packaged and sold by other companies as well.

You remove dirt by simply sliding the block back and forth along the track until the track shines. One word of caution here: Some cleaning blocks have a very harsh, coarse abrasive. While they may work well for removing dirt, they will scratch the tops of the rails. These scratches will catch dirt and make cleaning more difficult later. The block should leave the rails with a shiny, polished look. You could also use a very fine emery cloth or sandpaper—a 600 grit or smaller would be fine. Wrap a small piece around a wooden block and clean as you would with an eraser block.

If you have scratched the tops of your rails with a harsh eraser block, you can polish out the scratches with very fine emery cloth or Flex-i-grit sanding sheets.

Another problem with this type of track cleaning is the risk to lineside structures and equipment of having your hand down by the right-of-way. You can decrease this danger by attaching the block to a short stick so that your unprototypically large hand stays out of harm's way (fig. 5-5). It can also be difficult or impossible to clean hidden trackage, although even hidden trackage and trackage in tun-

nels should never be inaccessible for cleaning (or in case of derailments).

Another track-cleaning method is the use of liquid track cleaners. A variety of such cleaners are available along with a number of track-cleaning "systems" that produce mixed results. The most common liquid track-cleaning system uses some type of pad or cloth soaked with solvent. The modeler slides the wet pad along the rails by hand to soften and remove the dirt. Use of the wet pad is similar to that of the eraser pad. Compared to cleaning with a block, this system has benefits. The liquid system has no abrasives to scratch the rail surface, and its pad or cloth leaves no eraser-like residue on the right-of-way. There are, however, potential problems to using a pad and liquids. A sliding pad can snag trackwork such as switch points, frogs, and guardrails. Liquids can also be messy to apply. They should not run down the sides of the rail into the roadbed. This can stain the right-of-way or even loosen already secured ballast. You should not use any solvent-type material that can leave an oily residue behind. The residue may attract more dirt.

Another method of cleaning track with a liquid utilizes actual train operation to clean the rails. Several types of track-cleaning cars are available. They usually feature some type of pad that is located between the trucks and rests on the rails. The pad is wet with solvent and a locomotive pulls the car over the railroad. This sliding pad suffers the same problems as the manually operated one I just described; it can snag on sharp-ended guard rails and switch points.

Over the last several years Centerline Products has offered a unique car. The Rail Cleaner provides the benefits of a solvent cleaner and eliminates the problems of sliding a pad over switches and crossings. It features a heavy metal frame with a rectangular opening.

Fig. 5-3. An eraser-type cleaning block is a good way to remove larger accumulations of dirt and oxidation.

Fig. 5-4. Run the block along the inside of the rail on occasion. Dirt can accumulate here too.

Fig. 5-5. For difficult-to-reach or confined areas, attach the cleaning block to a stick with a screw or nail. It will keep large hands away from small details.

Inside the opening, a solid knurled brass piece of bar stock covered with a Handi-Wipe towel wet with Goo Gone solvent rolls along the rails. The idea is to run the car a number of times over the railroad. The solvent softens the dirt, and the same paper towel picks up the loosened dirt after several trips. When the towel becomes dirty, you replace it with another. After an initial cleaning, running the Rail Cleaner on a regular basis will prevent any significant buildup of dirt.

Using this car or system results in a so-called "wet" rail system. A small amount of the solvent remains on the rails and serves to slow oxidation, since the thin coating of liquid prevents oxygen from reaching the top rail surface. In my opinion this is probably the best method available to clean and maintain even the largest model railroad empire. Obviously, you'll have to run the car on all side and yard tracks on a regular basis to treat the entire railroad.

An older method of what could be called continuous cleaning uses a Masonite pad mounted under a piece of rolling stock. Figure 5-6 shows such a pad and the car underframe that goes with it. The Masonite, sliding over the rails, wipes the rails with every pass it makes.

In HO scale the pad can be about 1¼" wide, and the length is whatever will fit between the wheels of the car you intend to use. Use some sandpaper to roughen what will be the bottom of the pad. This will help remove dirt. To keep the pad properly positioned under the car, epoxy two 10d or 12d common nails to the top of the pad. Drill holes in the underframe of the car corresponding to the nails on the pad. When the epoxy has cured, slide the pad in place. The pad must have some freedom of movement so that any track irregularities do not cause problems. When such a pad is mounted under a boxcar, it is not very noticeable. Run the car regularly over your railroad to prevent the buildup of dirt. Occasionally remove the pad and scrape the accumulated

dirt from it. Sometimes the accumulated dirt actually starts to squeak or squeal slightly when the car is moving. This means that you should scrape off the dirt. While this setup may not be as effective as some of the newer track-cleaning systems, it is a cheap and easy way to remove dirt, and it can be built by anybody.

Whatever method of rail cleaning you choose, remember that you must do it regularly. If you do not operate your trains on a regular basis, clean your rails before you do any serious running to prevent major buildup on the wheels. Obviously, the frequency of track cleaning will depend on your circumstances. Experience will be your guide.

Clean the scenery. The same dust that coats your track coats your scale grass, trees, rocks, and other scenery as well. You can dust rocks and other such "hard" scenery in the same way as your structures. Just remember that any loose material will be sucked off the layout like the dust. While it is not necessary to use a mesh "capture" bag, you may want it for insurance, especially if you have small detail items and figures scattered around the layout.

Luckily, the foliage is so porous and tenuous that it can absorb a lot of dust before the dust shows. This is fortunate, because trying to remove any accumulation is difficult. Depending on how strongly your scenery material and foliage are secured, you may be able to tap them lightly with a small brush to dislodge some of the dust. Another possibility is to lightly dampen the foliage with a mist of water from a spray bottle (fig. 5-7). This will wash some of the dust off the outermost edges of your foliage and deposit it deeper into the material, making it less visible.

While I have used both of these methods to touch up scenery, I do not endorse either for general and universal use on a layout because they involve disturbing fragile items. They are, however, something for the

Fig. 5-6. A simple Masonite pad makes a respectable rail cleaner. Epoxy two nails to the pad and drill corresponding holes in the frame of a car.

modeler to think about. Whether you're able to use either method will depend on the type of scenery you built, how strong it is, and what materials you used. The tapping method is risky because it may break fragile foliage and trees. Spraying water on scenery secured with water-soluble adhesives is also risky. Too much water may dissolve the adhesive, resulting in defoliation of your scale forests and making your layout look as if a plague of scale locusts has descended on it. If you use water, try to avoid spraying it on buildings or other structures, since unsightly water spots can develop.

Water will most likely need more attention than any other type of scenery on your layout. The glossy water's surface will show not only dust but smudges and fingerprints. Your water will probably be the part of the scenery that people touch most, especially when newcomers visit. The glossiness and shininess of miniature rivers and ponds are fascinating. The temptation is more than most visitors can resist; they simply *must* touch the water.

You can usually clean any type of cast water with nothing more than a water-dampened cloth (fig. 5-8). Using a soft cloth, wipe the water surface gently, since the plastic surface can scratch. Nothing looks more unwaterlike than a scratch on a mirror-smooth expanse of water, whatever the scale. Should you have stubborn grease, fingerprints, or other dirt, dampen the soft cloth with a mild detergent or window cleaner and gently wipe away the deposits. Follow this with a water-dampened cloth to remove the loosened dirt and any soap residue. With proper care your water should continue to look as if it were just poured.

Clean the structures. Although it may not be noticeable on other scenery, a layer of dust can be very noticeable on structures. Some less ambitious modelers may claim that a layer of dust actually looks more

WORKBENCH TIP: A SLICK OIL TRICK

Apply clipper oil with a small applicator like a cotton swab. This will control the amount you apply.

Several years ago there were a number of articles and a lot of lively discussion about using Wahl hair clipper oil as a way to improve locomotive operation. The product was also supposed to decrease the number of times track had to be cleaned. The method is simple. After thoroughly cleaning the track and all wheels, apply a small amount of clipper oil to some type of applicator; my favorite is a Q-tip cotton swab. At intervals of several feet, rub the cloth along the rails for several inches, depositing a thin layer of oil. Run your trains to spread an even coat of this oil over all the trackage. The thin coat of oil serves as a barrier to slow oxidation of the rail surface, resulting in

longer periods of good performance, and thus extending the time between track cleanings. The trick to using this method successfully is to get the thinnest coat of oil possible on the rail surface. The danger is that an excessive amount of oil will act as a magnet for dirt and quickly turn both rail and wheels into an oily mess.

There has been little mention of this method in recent years, but there are modelers who have had success with this system and continue to use it. The potential problems caused by excessive application of oil make it a tricky proposition for the beginner or the careless.

realistic because it gives an overall weathering or blending effect. But the dust becomes strikingly apparent if someone runs a finger across a smooth, flat surface like a roof, leaving a nice trail. You can dust your structures with a small, soft brush. But brushing the dust away only moves it somewhere else. You should really remove it completely from the layout. You can do this by carefully following your brush with the hose of your vacuum cleaner (fig. 5-9) so that the vacuum sucks up the dislodged dust. The vacuum cleaner in effect acts like a miniature tornado on the layout.

Dusting may knock loose small pieces of the layout. To keep the vacuum cleaner from devouring them and other small, loose parts, place a piece of fine mesh material (fig. 5-10) somewhere in the vacuum-cleaning system to intercept these objects. A good place for this is between the end attachment and the hose. The mesh should be finer than the smallest pieces likely to be encountered but not so fine as to be plugged by dust and dirt. This method may be tedious and time-consuming, but there is no easier way to remove dust from items on a permanent layout. In larger scales you could use compressed air instead of a brush, but the air pressure could be damaging to delicate items.

For the purposes of such maintenance, it may be better to have as many items as possible removable from the layout. That way you can remove the items from the layout, dust them, and return them when clean. It would take a little planning, but it would make dusting the remaining items like roads and streets easier.

If you have a small, portable, or modular layout, you are fortunate. You can move the entire layout, or at least sections of it, to a place where the dust and dirt don't matter. In fact, on a nice breezy day you can let mother nature do your vacuuming

Fig. 5-7. A light mist of water will wash some of the surface dust deeper into the foliage, improving its appearance. Do not soak the foliage, or your adhesive may be weakened or dissolved.

Fig. 5-8. Clean the water on your layout with a soft, damp cloth. A little mild detergent should remove stubborn dirt. Do not press too hard, or you may scratch the water.

outdoors. Simply dust with your brush and the breeze will carry away the dust.

ADJUSTING TRACKWORK

Clean track is only part of the battle to keep trains running. You must maintain the track to certain tolerances in both gauge and surface for continuing smooth and trouble-free operation. While most track components, if properly installed, will give many years of reliable service, many outside forces are at work that can be a continuing source of problems. Use—but more likely, misuse—will cause operational problems with the track.

Another source of potential trouble is the support structure below the track. Wood is probably the primary material used for benchwork and subroadbed construction. By nature it reacts to changing climatic conditions, chiefly humidity and temperature. Expansion and contraction are the results of this reaction, and these forces can affect even the most carefully adjusted track. While extreme expansion or contraction may cause noticeable kinks or buckles in the track, most problems will be more subtle and not noticeable to the naked eye. Unfortunately, most mod-

elers wait until operational problems have developed before checking things out.

Even if things are running smoothly, the modeler should regularly run a track gauge over the right-of-way to locate potential trouble spots. You'll be able to find small irregularities and correct them before they become operational problems. While you could use the NMRA track gauge for this purpose, a better solution is to use a three-point gauge. These gauges, primarily made for those who handlay their track, are sold by several manufacturers. The advantage of using this type of gauge is that you can slide it continuously along the track and quickly find any gauge deviation. Three-point gauges are rail-code specific, so buy the proper size gauge or gauges if you have more than one size of rail. The gauges will not work over crossings or turnouts; here is where you'll use the NMRA gauge. In N scale a Micro-Trains coupler gauge will work, since one side has a track gauge. Side it along your track as shown in fig. 5-11.

When "patrolling" your track with the three-point gauge, you will very likely encounter tight spots in your trackage. This is usually no cause for concern unless you must lift the gauge off the rail to clear the spot. If that is the case, use an NMRA gauge to check the spot. If the track gauge is wide or narrow beyond the NMRA tolerance, adjust the track.

Handlaid track is easy to adjust. Exert corrective pressure on the side of the rail and drive several spikes into the ties along the defect until the gauge is correct (fig. 5-12). Commercial track is quite another matter. The nature of commercial track, with its rails molded into a hard plastic tie strip, makes gauge adjustments a significant undertaking. To adjust the gauge on this type of track, remove the molded-on spikes and any tie plate detail down to the level of the bottom of the rail for the length of the defect. You can do this with a no. 17 X-acto blade. Then you must secure the rail in proper gauge. It's best to use small spikes. Micro Engineering ¼" or ⁵⁄₁₆" Micro Spikes work well for this. First you'll have to drill holes through the ties, since it's impossible to drive the spikes through the tough plastic. Use a three-point track gauge to hold the rail in proper gauge and drill spike holes in at least every third or fourth tie right along the base of the rail (fig. 5-13). The size of the holes should be as close as possible to the size of spikes so they are a snug fit. This is necessary especially if you have a soft roadbed material, such as cork or Homasote, since these materials do not hold spikes securely enough on their own. If the spikes are a tight fit in the tie holes, they will hold the rail just fine. Use needle-nose pliers to push the spikes into place (fig. 5-14). If the spikes are a little loose, dip them in thickened cyanoacrylate and insert them, leaving the track gauge in place until the cyanoacrylate has set.

ADJUSTING TURNOUTS AND CROSSINGS

Turnouts or switches (the prototype term) are among the most troublesome pieces of trackage the modeler has to deal with. While the frog

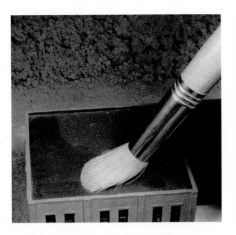

Fig. 5-9. Remove dust from structures with a soft brush. Follow the brush with a vacuum cleaner hose to suck up the dust, or you will just be moving it from one place to another on your layout.

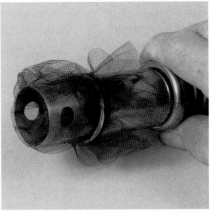

Fig. 5-10. Put fine lace or mesh cloth over the end of your vacuum-cleaner hose. Then you won't lose small items or have to dig them out of the collection bag.

and guard rails are a potential source of problems, once these items are properly adjusted, they usually behave themselves. It is the points, the movable sections of rail, that cause most of the grief.

The points are sections of rail that actually guide the train from one track to another. The name is self-explanatory: They are lengths of rail that taper to a nearly knifelike edge or point. This point is held against the stock, or outside, rail of a turnout, and the sharp edge guides the wheels away from the stock rail. Each normal turnout has two points that are held the proper distance apart by the throwbar. The throwbar moves and hold the points in the proper position, allowing the train to pass through the turnout in whatever direction it is set. The throwbar is connected to whatever mechanical means the modeler chooses to "throw" the points, either a hand throw or some type of remote control.

In order for the turnout points to function properly, you must maintain a number of critical adjustments. No single adjustment is more significant than the others; all are important.

Each point must fit snugly against the stock rail when the turnout is thrown in that direction. If

the fit isn't good, wheel flanges may "pick the point" and derail. Manufacturers handle this point rail–stock rail contact in one of two ways: They slightly notch the stock rail so that the point fits into the notch; or they leave the stock rail as is and shape the point rail so that it fits closely alongside the stock rail. The better turnouts do not notch the stock rail, at least not the head of the rail. The tip of the point should be as sharp as possible. If they are not, you should sharpen them. Figure 5-15 shows a rather blunt point that may cause problems. Improve a blunt end like this by filing the end to a sharper point. Figure 5-16 shows what part of the point to sharpen. A needle file works best to sharpen the end to the proper shape.

Dirt or a piece of ballast may also work its way between the two rails, preventing a tight fit (fig. 5-17). Check the area carefully for foreign material if problems start to occur at a particular turnout.

The opposite, or open, point must maintain adequate clearance between itself and the stock rail, so the wheels do not catch it and derail. While the NMRA does not have a recommended practice for this spacing, if you use the wider center flangeway nub on the NMRA gauge, the wheels will clear adequately. Commercial turnouts may vary in how they power the frog and point rails, so you must determine how yours are wired (fig. 5-18). If your turnouts are wired with the point rails connected to the frog, it means that both point rails are the polarity of the point rail in contact with the stock rail. The open point is the opposite polarity of the nearby stock rail. If there is only minimum clearance, the wheels receiving electricity from the stock rail may brush the opposite polarity point and cause an electrical short. The open point on such a turnout must have more clearance to prevent this. Unfortunately, there is no easy way to adjust this spacing on commercial turnouts. You'll have to modify the throwbar or make a new one.

The pivot point of the point rails can be another source of problems. On the prototype, there is no hinge or pivot. The point rails are continuous and are actually bent to move the points. Most, if not all, commercial turnouts have some form of pivot. Some work well, while others are loose and can cause gauge problems. There should be no sharp ends at the hinge point (fig. 5-19). It should be smooth. If the hinge is somewhat sloppy, the ends of the rail at the pivot point can move slightly out of alignment. This movement can allow an end of the pivot rail to catch a wheel flange and derail the car. If the movement of the rail does not exceed track gauge tolerances, you can file slightly the corners of the ends of the rail at the joint to remove the square end, thus keeping wheel flanges from catching the corners. If the rail movement exceeds the track gauge tolerances, you'll have to either tighten or adjust the hinging mechanism.

It is possible to adjust or tighten some hinges. On turnouts that use a rivet as a hinge pivot, drive long spikes or a track nail into the center of the rivet. Push them into the roadbed to take out some of the slack

Fig. 5-11. The track gauge on the side of the Micro-Trains N scale coupler gauge is great for "patrolling" your track. In HO scale a three-point track gauge used for handlaying track serves the same purpose.

Fig. 5-12. Adjust handlaid track in the same way as you laid it. Use small spikes to hold any gauge adjustments.

(fig. 5-20). If you use cork roadbed, the nail or spike should be long enough to reach through the cork into the more solid subroadbed. Carefully set the nail or spike until most of the slack is gone, but not so much that the hinge cannot easily pivot or that the rail is pulled down, causing a surface problem. Beyond this, things can get complicated.

Each point rail must also be in correct gauge throughout its length when the turnout is thrown for its direction. Use your NMRA gauge to check this. Adjust any gauge differences by carefully pushing on the side of the rail in the direction that the rail should move (fig. 5-21). You should hold the ends of the rail at the throwbar and hinge so the pressure does not damage the rail attachments at these points. The rail may be quite springy, so you may have to bend it quite a bit before the rail will "give" enough.

The frog is another source of problems. There are no moving parts here, so it is just a matter of making sure everything is correctly adjusted and secure. The NMRA gauge is again the tool for the job. First, check to make sure the rail gauge is correct throughout the turnout. Make any necessary adjustment before pro-

ceeding. Use the track-adjustment procedures described earlier in this chapter if needed. Now use the flangeways side of the gauge. The instructions that came with the gauge describe and illustrate how to check spacing of the wing and guard rail and the depth of the flangeway. If you don't have the NMRA sheet, the two outside nubs must fit into the frog flangeways as shown in fig. 5-22, but the wider center nub must not fit into the opening (fig. 5-23). If you find problems, adjust the guard or wing rails accordingly.

Adjust the guard rails in one of two ways. If you adjust them in place, the results will not be as good as if you reposition them. You can open a narrow flangeway by filing the side of the guard rail until the gauge fits. The danger is that while removing material from the side of the guard rail, you will also remove material from the side of the stock rail, leaving a bow in the rail. Correct a flangeway that is too wide by cementing a thin piece of styrene to the side of the guard rail with cyanoacrylate or epoxy. This is an easy quick fix, but if an end should come loose, it could foul the flangeway and cause derailments.

The wing rails are part of the frog casting, and moving them is a lot of

Fig. 5-13. Plastic ties are tough. In order to adjust the gauge, you'll have to drill holes for the spikes through the ties.

Fig. 5-14. Spikes should fit tightly into the holes. Insert them with needle-nose pliers.

RAIL AND TIE REPAIR

Fig. 1. Repair a horizontal kink in a rail by grasping the rail on each side of the kink with needle-nose pliers and bending the rail back to position. A sharp kink may be difficult to remove completely.

Fig. 2. Push down on the rail equally on both sides of the kink; locking-jaw pliers do the job here. The lighter the rail, the less pressure you'll have to apply to straighten the kink.

work. If the flangeway is too narrow, use a needle file and remove material from the side of the wing rail to fit the gauge (fig. 5-24). Be careful while you're doing this, because the maximum width of the flangeway must not allow the center nub of the gauge to fit between the rails. If the frog flangeway is too wide, it is possible to narrow the gap by cementing a thin strip of styrene to the insides of the wing rails with cyanoacrylate or epoxy.

Check the flangeway depth as well (fig. 5-25). The nubs on the NMRA gauge should not bottom out in the flangeway. If they do, check for dirt buildup or foreign material. If there is no dirt, remove some material from the bottom of the flangeway; otherwise, locomotive and car

You can damage track in a number of ways. You can drop heavy things on it, causing bends or kinks in the rail. In extreme cases this can damage the ties as well.

Regardless of the source of the damage, you'll have to repair the track structure before you can resume proper operation. If you are well along with a layout and have already ballasted the track, you may want to repair the damage in place rather than cut out and replace a section of track. If the rail has been bent or kinked, the easiest solution would be to straighten it in place. It may be possible to straighten a smooth bend by putting pressure on the outside of the bend and pushing until the rail is back in gauge—the lighter the rail, the less pressure you'll need.

A kink in the rail may be more difficult to remove. Use a pair of needle-nose pliers to fix horizontal kinks. Grasp the rail on each side of the kink and bend it back

into shape (fig. 1). If possible, use smooth-jaw pliers, since the grooves in a typical pair of pliers may chew up the rail head. It may be difficult to remove all of the kink, but by carefully positioning the pliers, you may succeed. A vertical kink, caused by a hard blow from above, is more difficult to remove. If possible, pry the rail up under the kink so it is slightly above the ties, exert pressure on each side of the kink, and push down (fig. 2).

If the damage was severe enough to depress the ties, you may be able to place thin shims between the ties and the rail to support it. Be careful not to shim too much and cause a high spot in the track. When the shims are properly in place, secure them with a small drop of cyanoacrylate adhesive or five-minute epoxy for a stronger repair. After the cement has cured, paint the repaired section to match the surrounding track to mask the shims.

Fig. 5-15. A blunt end on the tip of a point rail can catch wheel flanges and cause derailments.

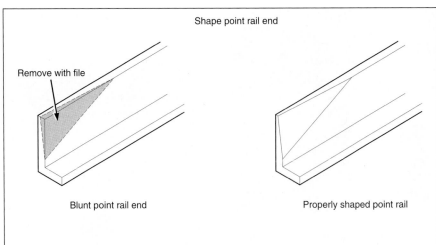

Shape point rail end

Remove with file

Blunt point rail end

Properly shaped point rail

Fig. 5-16. File blunt ends as shown to decrease the chance of catching a flange.

Fig. 5-17. If a point rail will not seat tightly against the stock rail, check the area between the stock rail and point rail for stray ballast or other obstructions that may prevent proper operation.

wheels will bounce over the flangeway and possibly cause a derailment. The side of a needle file works well to deepen a flangeway. In HO scale a piece of hacksaw blade is the perfect flangeway width and also works well. Use a piece to saw a deeper flange-

way if needed (fig. 5-26). Check your progress frequently, and go no deeper than necessary.

ADJUSTING SWITCH MACHINES AND GROUND THROWS

There are two ways of throwing your model switch points: by remote control or by hand throws. Regardless of the method you choose, the object is to move one point away from the stock rail while pushing the other point against the opposite stock rail and holding it securely. Maintenance of these items is mostly a matter of keeping them in proper adjustment and free of dirt and debris.

Hand or ground throws are easy to adjust. The most important concern is that the points must be pushed securely against the stock rail when thrown for a particular direction of travel. If the points come up short, it is obvious what will happen—your train will "split a switch." If one of your points starts coming up short, there are several possible explanations. Some ballast or other debris may have worked loose and found its way into the point, throwbar area, or ground throw mechanism itself. Remove the ground throw and slide the throwbar by hand. If it binds or if the points do not seat properly to the stock rail, there is some foreign material where it

shouldn't be. Removing the material can be a little tricky if it is not visible, since it may be wedged alongside or under the throwbar. The best way to dislodge the material is with air. If you have an air compressor or some other source of compressed air, blow it into the throwbar area while you work the throwbar back and forth. Do not use high pressure, or you may scour ballast from your right-of-way. If this doesn't work, keep working the throwbar back and forth. The material should eventually roll out from wherever it is hiding. If the material is in the ground throw mechanism, either find it and physically pick it out or work the mechanism until it dislodges. After removing any foreign material, reinstall the ground throw.

If the ground throw simply needs readjustment, move it in the proper direction and secure it again. If you use screws to attach your ground throws and there is no allowance for adjustment, remove it and use a round needle file to elongate the mounting hole in the direction needed (fig. 5-27). Replace the ground throw, position it properly, and tighten the screws.

Maintenance and adjustment of remote turnout mechanisms is more complicated because you have to deal with a mechanical, electrical, or pneumatic mechanism. If you're having problems with the point throw, disconnect the throwing mechanism and check the points and throwbar for foreign material as I explained previously. Next, check your source of remote power. Is electricity or air reaching the mechanism? If not, check your power supply or control panel for proper operation. If it checks out okay, begin looking at the mechanism.

How to adjust and maintain mechanical throws depends on what type of mechanism you use. Whether you have a choke cable or a lever-type mechanism, there should be some form of adjustment to shorten or lengthen the linkage. Use this adjustment to correct any point throw problems. If there is no type of adjustment in the linkage, you may have to bend part of the linkage physically to adjust it.

Maintaining mechanical remote throws chiefly involves not allowing anything to interfere with the linkage. Most, if not all, of these remotes are located below the layout, so keep wire or other layout components that could interfere with them well away or properly secured. Avoid applying oil to any sliding or moving parts if possible. Over time the oil can attract dirt, which can dry and harden, causing binding. Perhaps the most important tip is to use a light hand when operating these types of remotes. Whether they have some form of stops or other method of limiting travel, do not use excessive force. You are not shifting a semi tractor.

Dealing with electric remote controls is more complicated. There are several available methods of throwing points. Probably the most widely used remote control for the casual modeler is the Atlas twin-coil switch machine. This item comes standard or can be added to their line of turnouts. Several other manufacturers also offer similar units for their lines of track switches. They are self-contained units that use a twin magnetic coil and simple lever to throw points.

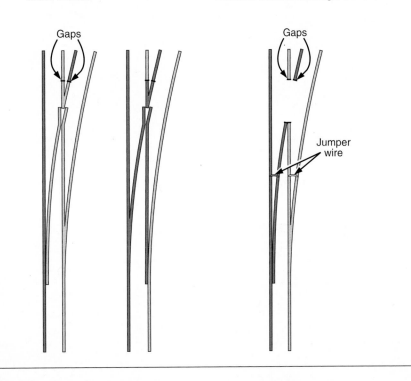

Point rails are fed power by contact with stock rail. If the gap between the open point rail and the stock rail isn't wide enough, a metal wheel may touch the inside of the point rail and cause a short.

Point rails are gapped before the frog and are powered from a jumper wire to the stock rail. Same polarity stock and point rails prevent shorting. Frog is dead but can be powered by switch in turnout throwing mechanism.

Gaps

Gaps

Jumper wire

Fig. 5-18. Point rail wiring options

Whether they are mounted on top of or under the layout, the operation is the same. Unfortunately, there is little the modeler can do to maintain or adjust these units because the working components are enclosed and the cover is secured with rivets. A common problem is that foreign material may find its way into the open end and keep the mechanism from operating properly. If you suspect that this may be the cause of your problem, remove the unit and work the mechanism manually. Hold the unit with the opening down so any material that is dislodged can fall out. Do not apply any type of oil to the unit—it will only attract dirt and gum up the mechanism. If this fails to solve the problem, you'll probably have to replace the unit.

Fig. 5-19. Check the point rail pivot point for tightness and for any sharp edges that may catch wheel flanges.

Small nail driven into
point rail pivots

Fig. 5-20. Tighten a loose pivot point on an Atlas turnout by driving a small nail into the rivet.

Fig. 5-21. For reliable operation check the rail gauge at a number of points. The point rails are especially vulnerable to gauge problems because they are moving parts.

Fig. 5-22. Use the pair of narrow nubs on the NMRA gauge to check the guard and wing rails for proper spacing.

Fig. 5-23. Use the center nub to check for excess spacing. The nub should not fit in the guard rail or wing rail gap.

When the model railroader goes beyond "snap-track" turnouts, there are a number of different kinds of switch machines and mounting options. Each modeler will make his or her own choice, depending on individual preferences and circumstances.

Other manufacturers make their own versions of the twin-coil switch machine that are intended to be mounted under the layout. The bet-ter ones have stronger components and have a way to adjust the throwbar linkage. One disadvantage of twin-coil machines is that they move the points in a quick, sharp snap that can loosen stock rails and knock point or stock rails out of adjustment.

There are several "slow motion" switch machines that move the points in a slower, more prototypical man-ner. The slower throw speed of these machines is easier on the track structure. One type uses a motor and screw drive that moves a pivoting point lever. The point lever is a flexible-spring wire linkage that will hold the points against the stock rail when thrown. A similar design uses a gear drive to move the point lever. Another type utilizes what is known as a stall motor. This is a larger motor that uses a continuous low voltage to move and then hold points in the desired position. You make any nec-essary adjustment by repositioning the unit slightly or by using the adjustment provided by slotted screw holes (if the machine has them).

A totally different type of switch throw utilizes air to throw the points. While this system allows the modeler to throw turnouts without running wires to the turnout, air lines must be run instead. The air-operated compo-nents will probably require less main-tenance than electrical components, but may require wiring for signal and turnout indicators.

Each of these systems has its own particular maintenance require-ments, and the manufacturers will

Fig. 5-24. To open a tight flangeway use a flat needle file and remove excess material from the sides of the wing or guard rail only.

Fig. 5-25. Check the frog depth with one of the nubs on the NMRA gauge. The center nub in the frog opening shows the correct depth.

Fig. 5-26. Deepen a flangeway with a flat needle file or a piece of hacksaw blade, which fortunately is the width of the flangeway.

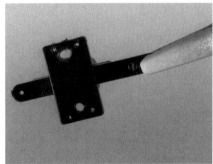

Fig. 5-27. Elongating the mounting holes can adjust a ground throw somewhat.

most likely support them with replacement parts. High-quality switch machines come with a parts list and instructions regarding any required or suggested maintenance. Follow those instructions for best results.

Another potential problem in dealing with remote-control turnouts is the control itself. Many turnouts are thrown with some type of push-button control. The contact points of

these push buttons can become pitted after a period of time. Each time a contact is made, a small spark burns a tiny pit into each surface. Over time this arcing will may cause a layer of burned material that actually insulates the metal contact points, making electrical contact difficult or impossible. If the contact points are accessible, sand them smooth with fine emery cloth to

remove the insulating material and pits. The switch will work fine again. If the points are not accessible, you'll have to take the switch apart and clean it or replace it.

There may also be contact points on the switch machines themselves. They are used for lighted position and signal system indicators. While they are not subject to pitting like the switch throw points, dirt can accumulate on the contact points and cause contact problems. Use very fine emery cloth to clean the dirt and oxidation. My favorite method is a four-grit nail file. Use a coarser grit to remove any oxidation

FROG REPAIR

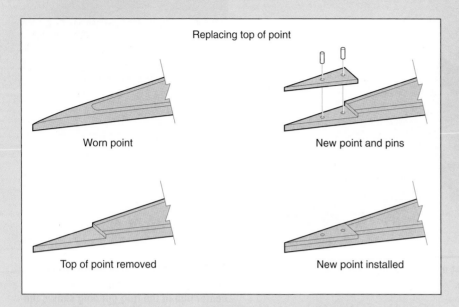

Replacing top of point

Worn point

New point and pins

Top of point removed

New point installed

The plastic frog on some turnouts can become worn or damaged and result in constant problems. Rather than replacing the entire turnout, make a metal cap for the turnout. Follow the sequence of drawings that illustrate this process.

The frog area of some turnouts may be susceptible to damage or wear, especially if the point of the frog is plastic. This is common on some "train set" switches. If wear is a problem, or if the point has been damaged in some manner, it will have to be repaired to restore reliable operation. You may not even have an operational problem. You may just want to replace the plastic portion of the frog to prevent such a problem or to power the frog.

Replacing the top of the point is the easiest repair. Sheet brass is the easiest metal to work with. Obviously, the thickness of the metal will have to be at least the thickness of the amount of the material you intend to remove. It is best to remove the material right down to the bottom of the flange-

way. Use the existing point as an example and shape the new point to exactly the same angle with a file. Now remove the section of the point that you intend to replace. It may be a little tricky to get between the wing rails, but once you have removed most of the point, you can scrape off the remaining material with the end of a no. 17 blade. Do not remove the plastic point all the way up to where the rails diverge. The plastic point insulates the two rails from each other. If your metal repair plate makes contact with either of the rails there will be a short circuit. Only if you intend to power your frog should the plate touch the rails, and then you'll have to cut a gap in the rails beyond the point area. Fit the new piece into the prepared opening.

Don't worry if the metal extends above the height of the other rails—you'll correct this later.

Use an epoxy-type adhesive to secure the plate. Any five-minute brand should do. First, drill several small holes into the flangeway area that the new plate will cover. The epoxy will ooze into these holes to help secure the new piece. To make an even stronger bond, drill several small holes through the new metal plate—a hole about .030" would be good. This hole size corresponds to Detail Associates .028" brass wire. Mix and apply the epoxy to the bottom of the new piece and set it in place. A little epoxy should ooze out all around the piece. After it has cured, run the .030" drill bit through the metal holes and drill all the way through the plastic portion of the turnout. Take an equal number of short pieces of .028" brass wire, dip them in a little epoxy, and insert them into the holes. Don't worry if a little wire extends from the top of the frog. Again, let everything cure. Now trim the end of the wire as close to the plate as possible. Then use a large flat mill file and file the new point down even with the rest of the tops of the rail. Also trim away the epoxy that oozed out into the flangeways. Do this with a knife or, in HO scale, with a short section of hacksaw blade, which is the same width as the flangeway. Use an NMRA gauge to check for proper flange width and depth, then roll some cars through the turnout to check for proper operation.

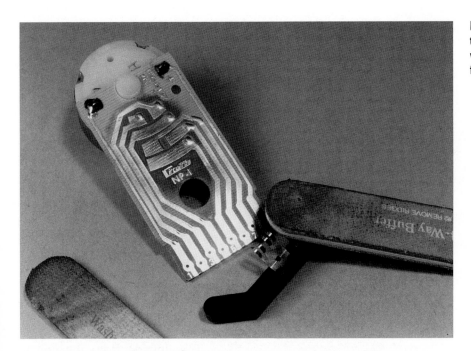

Fig. 5-28. Clean the contact points on turnout indicators and switches with very fine emery cloth, or in this case a four-way nail buffer.

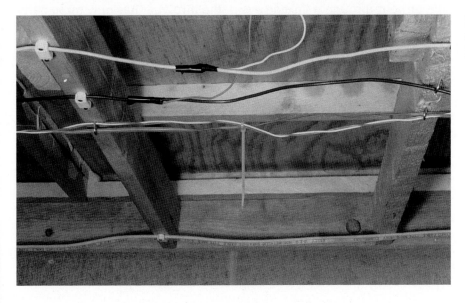

Fig. 5-29. Bundle wiring neatly and secure it to the underside of the layout to prevent damage.

or burned material and work down to the finest grade, which will polish the contacts. Some ground throws also have contact points that are used for position indication. Clean them in the same way.

MAINTAINING ELECTRICAL STANDARDS

Electrical maintenance is probably not an accurate term, especially compared to such ongoing functions as track and locomotive maintenance. It should be considered an ongoing project. Electrical maintenance is more like maintaining a standard than like cleaning and oiling. If you wire your layout carefully and route and secure all wires neatly, maintenance should be minimal. If you do it in a slipshod way and buck it together, the time you spend beneath the layout fixing may be substantial.

When you see problems, deal with them as soon as possible. Tighten loose connections properly. Resolder loose or cracked solder joints; don't ignore them until they break off completely. Clean any contact points that are causing problems when you first notice them (fig. 5-28). Bundle low-hanging or loose wires under your layout or secure them properly so they don't catch on something and come loose (fig. 5-29). Similarly bundle or secure the wiring for new components. Cover bare wire or damaged insulation immediately with electrical tape or, better yet, replace it.

Attach a spade or ring terminal (fig. 5-30) to the end of any wire that is not soldered to a connection or

SWITCH MACHINE REPAIR

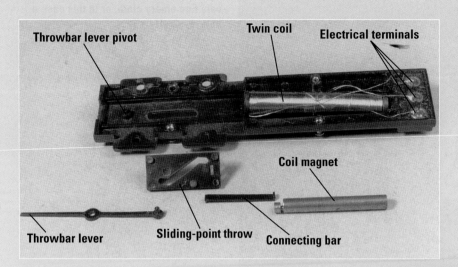

Throwbar lever pivot
Twin coil
Electrical terminals
Coil magnet
Throwbar lever
Sliding-point throw
Connecting bar

Other than the coils, the mechanical portion of the remote-control turnout is simple.

On larger layouts you can spend a lot of time repairing switch machines. Because the machines vary so widely, there is not enough room in this book to describe all the problems that can afflict them.

To simplify matters, there are basically two types of machines, the twin-coil and the slow-motion. The twin-coil machine uses a momentary burst of electricity to energize one of the coils and throw the turnout through a linkage system. The slow-motion machine uses a motor and some form of gear reduction to turn a pivot. A flexible wire usually connects the pivot to the turnout throwbar.

There are a number of types of twin-coil machines. Some of the higher-quality and more expensive machines are very reliable, and spare parts are usually available from the manufacturer.

Probably the most-used type of remote-control switch machine is made by Atlas. While the unit is a good value for the money, it does not lend itself to easy repair, which means that a modeler often considers it a throw-away item when it breaks. Don't throw anything away—at least, not without trying to fix it. If you have an Atlas machine that does not work and you want to attempt a repair, the first thing you must do is remove the rivets. Use a drill with a bit slightly larger than the rivet and drill one side of the flange off the rivet. Turn the machine on its back and remove the cover.

The linkage from the coil to the throwbar has only three parts. Two are fragile and are easy to replace. You can replace the connector bar with one made of brass. You can replace the throwbar lever with one made from brass sheet and a piece of brass screw soldered to one end. Use the old part as a pattern. It doesn't have to look perfect, but the critical dimensions should be very close.

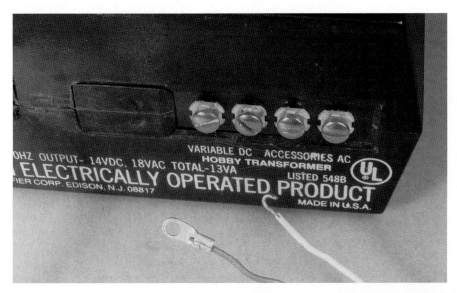

Fig. 5-30. Looping the end of a wire to connect it to a screw terminal may work on this power pack. But a more positive and reliable means of connecting wire to a such a device is to use a ring or spade terminal.

terminal or is intended to be removable. This provides a more reliable means of securing a wire to a screw terminal. Although you usually attach most spade or ring terminals by inserting the wire and crimping the end, you should also solder all such connections to provide positive contact. Crimped wires can come loose or pull out.

Never run low-voltage wire alongside 110-volt house wiring. These wires should never touch each other. If house wiring or 110-volt wire serving the layout is damaged in any way, you must repair it immediately. Such problems can result in fires or even electrocution. If you are not experienced in working with 110-volt house wiring, seek the help of someone who is or hire a professional. It makes no sense to endanger property and lives in the pursuit of a hobby.

Although layout maintenance is not difficult, it does require an investment of time and a few basic mechanical skills. The most important requirement is the discipline needed to deal with items on a regular basis or, at the very least, at the first sign of trouble. The time and effort will be rewarded with interest because the result will be a smoothly running layout that will be satisfying to operate and a joy to share and show to others.

REPLACING LAYOUT WIRING

The requirements for wiring a layout are a function of its size and complexity. Consequently, small layouts are sometimes wired better than their larger counterparts. In the haste to get larger layouts operational, layout builders may run temporary wires with the intention of upgrading later. All too often, later becomes quite a long time. Since wiring is usually hidden, it is usually left alone—as long as current flows through it to the proper location. It is out of sight and out of mind. The problem is that temporary usually means that almost anything goes. Wires run everywhere, light gauge wire is substituted for the recommended gauge wire, connections are sometimes just twisted together and not properly insulated, to name a few pitfalls. While even the best-wired layouts may experience electrical problems, subpar wiring will almost certainly plague operations. High voltage drops in long runs of light wire will cause widely varying train speeds in certain areas. Loose or open connections and, even worse, shorts will occur far too often. You could even cause damage to the state-of-the-art circuitry found in new motive power.

Maybe your layout was wired properly, everything neatly and carefully done, and has operated with few problems since its completion. That may not be good enough anymore. With the rapid development of electronic devices, especially Digital Command Control or DCC for train and layout operation, wiring needs to be of even higher standards for optimum performance.

If you plan to upgrade your wiring for a DCC system, or just for more reliable conventional operation, you might be better off to replace everything rather than sections or pieces of wiring. A clean start will eliminate the temptation to cut corners or only do the worst sections. Everything can be done to the same standards. The subject of layout wiring is quite broad and beyond the scope of this book, but a book such as *Easy Model Railroad Wiring* by Andy Sperandeo covers the subject well.

PUT YOUR WIRING TO THE TEST

A simple automotive circuit tester will work well for detecting electrical current in track or any other wiring.

More important than how damage occurs is what immediate effects or potential problems will be the result of damaged wire. Fixing a damaged wire is usually quite easy.

Finding the source or location of the problem can be the difficult part.

An important part of troubleshooting involves testing. It is easy to test whether or not power is reaching the rails—just set a locomotive on the rails and turn on the power. But how can a modeler check whether power is reaching various terminals on and under the layout? A simple automotive circuit tester will work well as a power indicator. A small alligator clip on one end and a pointed probe on the other end make it easy and quick to check for current in a circuit. For a buck or two you can make your own tester by soldering short pieces of wire to the terminals of a 12- to 16-volt flashlight bulb. If you want to get fancy, you can also add an alligator clip. If you plan to get more involved in electronics, it may be worth while to invest in a multitester. Such a unit not only indicates the presence of electricity in a circuit, it also shows voltage. You can adjust the voltage scale to cover a wide range from fractions of a volt, usable for electronic devices, all the way up to house current voltage. A complete set of instructions comes with such devices, explaining their use in detail.

Suppliers and Manufacturers

A-Line
Division of Proto Power West
P. O. Box 2701
Carlsbad, CA 92018

Athearn
19010 Laurel Park Rd.
Compton, CA 90222

Bachmann Industries
1400 E. Erie Ave.
Philadelphia, PA 19124

Caboose Industries
1861 Ridge Dr.
Freeport, IL 61032

Cal-Scale
P. O. Box 322
Montoursville, PA 17754

Centerline Products
18409 Harmony Rd.
Marengo, IL 60152

Con-Cor International
8101 E. Research Ct.
Tuscon, AZ 85710

Detail Associates
P. O. Box 5357
San Luis Obispo, CA 93403

Details West
P. O. Box 61
Corona, CA 91718

Evergreen Scale Models
12808 N. E. 125th Way
Kirkland, WA 98034

Grandt Line Products
1040-B Shary Ct.
Concord, CA 94518

Hobbytown of Boston
P. O. Box 5135
Hollywood, FL 33083

K&S Engineering
6917 W. 59th St.
Chicago, IL 60638

Kadee Quality Products
673 Ave. C
White City, OR 97503

Kato U.S.A.
100 Remington Rd.
Schaumburg, IL 60173

La Belle Industries
P. O. Box 328
Bensenville, IL 60106

Mantua Industries
P. O. Box 10
Woodbury Heights, NJ 08097

Mascot Precision Tools
750 Washington Ave.
Carlstadt, NJ 07072

Micro Engineering
1120 Eagle Rd.
Fenton, MO 63026

Micro-Mark
340 Snyder Ave.
Berkeley Heights, NJ 07922

Model Power
180 Smith St.
Farmingdale, NY 11735

NMRA
4121 Cromwell Rd.
Chatanooga, TN 37421

NorthWest Short Line
P. O. Box 423
Seattle, WA 98111

Overland Models
3808 W. Kilgore Ave.
Muncie, IN 47304

Plastruct
1020 S. Wallace Pl.
City of Industry, CA 91748

Precision Scale
P. O. Box 278
Stevensville, MT 59870

Radio Shack
900 E. Northside Dr.
Fort Worth, TX 76102
(many locations nationwide)

Smokey Valley Railroad Products
P. O. Box 339
Plantersville, MS 38862

Stewart Hobbies
P. O. Box 341
Chalfont, PA 18914

Testor Corp.
620 Buckbee St.
Rockford, IL 61104

Tomar Industries
9520 E. Napier Rd.
Benton Harbor, MI 49022

Wm. K. Walthers
P. O. Box 3039
Milwaukee, WI 53201

Woodland Scenics
P. O. Box 98
Linn Creek, MO 65052

Xuron Corp.
60 Industrial Park Rd.
Saco, ME 04072

Index